Sex and the Church

SEX AND THE CHURCH

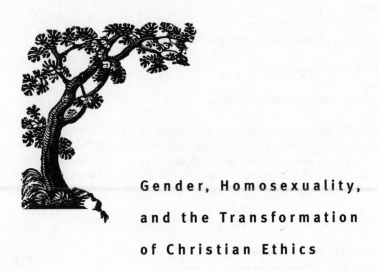

Gender, Homosexuality, and the Transformation of Christian Ethics

KATHY RUDY

Beacon Press

Beacon Press
25 Beacon Street
Boston, Massachusetts 02108-2892

Beacon Press books
are published under the auspices of
the Unitarian Universalist Association of Congregations.

An earlier version of part of chapter 4 was published as " 'Where Two or More Are Gathered':
Using Gay Communities as a Model for Christian Sexual Ethics" in *Theology and Sexuality* 4
(March 1996): 81–101. An earlier version of chapters 5 and 6 was published as "The Social
Construction of Sexual Identity and the Ordination of 'Practicing' Homosexuals" in *The Journal
of Religious Ethics* 25, no. 1 (Spring 1997). The author is grateful for permission to reprint.

02 01 00 99 98   8 7 6 5 4 3 2

Text design by Jeannet Leendertse
Composition by Wilsted & Taylor

Library of Congress Cataloging-in-Publication Data
Rudy, Kathy.
     Sex and the church : gender, homosexuality, and the transformation of Christian ethics /
Kathy Rudy.
        p.   cm.
     ISBN 0-8070-1034-0 (cloth)
     ISBN 0-8070-1035-9 (paper)
     1. Homosexuality—Religious aspects—Christianity.   2. Sex role—Religious aspects—
Christianity.   3. Sex—Religious aspects—Christianity.   4. Sexual ethics.   5. Christian
ethics.   I. Title.
BR115.H6R83   1997
241'.66—dc21   96-50190

for Jan

Contents

Acknowledgments

I am indebted to the people and institutions that supported the intellectual work behind this book. The book was conceived while I was a postdoctoral fellow at Princeton's Center for the Study of American Religion, and the guidance of many seminar members—especially Bob Wuthnow, John Wilson, and Nancy Ammerman—was extremely important. My colleagues in the women's studies program at Duke—Jean O'Barr, Nancy Rosebaugh, Sarah Hill, Cynthia Banks-Glover, and Vivian Robinson—provided the intellectual support and material conditions for me to write as well as teach. Finally, a group of graduate and divinity students who met with me in an independent study forum in the spring of 1995—including Dean Blackburn, Liz Waters, Sandy Malasky, Diana Swancutt, and Seth Persily—helped me clarify the arguments in the later parts of the book. I am grateful for their insights and convictions.

But this book is not only about intellectual work. The emotional support I received before and throughout graduate school enabled me to critique the sexist, homophobic rhetoric of the Christian church, of which I am a part. I want to thank the many people who helped me to form and accept my identity as a lesbian, as well as those people who challenged me to see the value in moving beyond such categories. Kathy Lanier, Judi Clark, Mary McClintock-Fulkerson, Liz Clark, Stanley Hauerwas, Claudia Koonz, Irene Silverblatt, and many others supported me through the many phases of "coming out," and Eve Sedgwick, especially, helped me figure out what "coming out" could possibly mean. Susan Worst, my editor at Beacon, read and edited every word of this book. As my relationship with Beacon Press continues, I am delighted to find in Susan not only an excellent editor but a good friend as well.

For many years, my life was primarily defined by my relationships with women. Perhaps the most surprising gift I have received in writing this book has been a new appreciation for the lives and work of certain men. Through these new friendships, I have realized that separatist politics are often not only politically divisive, but also terribly isolating. Without the support, insights, and example of Randy Styres, Scott Tucker, Bob Goss, Michael Moon, and Jonathan Goldberg, this would be a very different book. I thank them, and continue to grow in my relationships with them.

Finally, more than anyone else, one person inspired me to write this book: my partner Janice Radway. The life we have led together for almost a decade now is rich and good, and no authority in any church, anywhere, can alter that. By loving me so well, she teaches me to have faith in myself, a faith that has only strengthened my relationship with God, and continues to make me hope that we can find God somewhere in this institution called church.

The issue of homosexuality threatens to divide Christian churches today in much the way that slavery did 150 years ago. Should "practicing" Christian homosexuals, bisexuals, and transgendered people be allowed to serve as ordained ministers? Should the unions of gay and lesbian couples be recognized as legitimate marriages in the eyes of God? These and other questions rend our congregations, our denominations, and sometimes even our families. One side asserts that people should be welcomed into our churches, into the ministry, and into our understanding of the American family regardless of their sexual orientation; the other side insists that any sexual preference other than heterosexuality is a sin and should be proscribed by all faithful Christians. No apparent solution to these disagreements lies on the horizon.

This book offers new ways to think about this stalemate. I believe we Christians are in desperate need of revitalization, both on issues related to homosexuality and on the related topics of gender and sexual ethics. But before we begin, we need a better, deeper understanding of contemporary Christian beliefs about homosexuality, sexual ethics, and women's role in the church. What questions are being asked, and which are left unasked? How is the debate about issues of gender and sex for Christians being framed, and is that framework in keeping with church tradition? What positions have our forebears taken on these issues, and why? This book will take up these questions.

I believe we must begin with the public words and works of the Christian Right—and in particular the logic and assertions associated with the family values campaign—in order to understand how the agenda and tone of contemporary Christian politics evolved. The family values campaign has resonated with a broad spectrum of Christians in America. However, although it makes important links between Christians of different races and classes, I will suggest that it does so by deepening the already troubled divisions between male and female Christians and between gay Christians and straight. I will show how the family values campaign is imbued with both homophobia and sexism, and demonstrate that these two oppressions are intrinsically and necessarily related. Specifically, we cannot understand the Right's homophobia until we uncover the deep commitment conservative Christianity has to nineteenth-century gender roles.

In this book, I suggest that mainline and progressively minded Christians should combat the sexism and homophobia of the Right's agenda by examining and moving beyond our commitment to the structure of family, by moving beyond gender and sexual identity politics, and by reconstructing a church politic based on Christian community. By applying contemporary queer theories to Christian theology, I argue that the church is the ideal location for questioning such institutions as the nuclear, heterosexual family. We are a people founded on the community called church; we understand ourselves within that community to constitute the Body of Christ. More strongly, I believe that our Christian commitment to God manifests itself first and foremost through our commitment to community. I argue that a more faithful and more radical sexual ethic can stem from grounding our ideas first and foremost in this community. By placing our commitment to community above and before any involvement in the local or nuclear family, we can develop an ethic that is not only more friendly to all sorts of sexual minorities, but also more faithful to the tradition of Christian community.

I will suggest throughout this work that sexuality is a site of spiritual and communal possibility, a way to proclaim the gospel and remember the call of Christ. Part of the reason that Christians have had a difficult time discussing sex (both heterosexual as well as homosexual) is because we intuit that something important—something almost beyond words—happens during sexual activity. On a deep level, we know that sex is a powerful component of many of our lives, and that it can have a connection to life's ultimate meaning which, for Christians, involves God. Lacking the language to discuss these connections, we allow ourselves—as I will display in chapters 2 and 3—to be captured by legalistic formulas prescribing narrow conditions for legitimate sex.

In the second part of this book, I will suggest that this is the wrong way to think about the relationship between sex, God, and the Christian church, or to understand what our genders and sexual preferences have to do with our relationships with God and with each other. I will argue that for Christians to build a viable community in the next century, we must discuss the philosophical and cultural presuppositions behind our understandings of moral and immoral sex. These discussions of sexual ethics not only respond to the call to alleviate oppression (in this case of women and gays), they also enable us to discuss the spiritual, elusive part of the Christian summons, how to treat our bodies as if they were spirit, how to embody the remembrance of Jesus. One of the costs of our inability as Christians to discuss sexual matters has been that the spiritual dimension of sex has all but disappeared. We do not see sex as being about the business of Christian community and loving God; rather we act as if it is too private to discuss. In our refusal to discuss the connection between sexuality and spirituality, we lose the ability to understand the Christian possibilities involved in the act of sex. In this book, I argue that we must understand our desire to be united with others through sexual acts also as the desire to be united with God. I will suggest that we must move away from the rule-based ethics we inherited from the nineteenth century into an era in which discussions of sex include and indeed are about God.

I use the idea that sex, God, and church are intricately intertwined as a criterion to judge the adequacy of Christian politics. And, as one might expect, I find enormous room for growth in the church today. However, I find this potential not just in the Christian Right, but also among some who favor "homosexual" membership in the church, as long as those homosexuals behave like heterosexuals. What we need, I argue, is not to adapt existing structures and categories to include lesbians, gay men, and bisexuals, but to rethink our vision of Christian community entirely by listening to the Word and Spirit of God. Using insights based in both gay practice and gay theory, I criticize (in chapters 4 and 5) the church-based movements for gay marriage and gay ordination because, in my view, both of these demands rely on outdated and oppressive categories. If the new creation of Christ calls us to organize our lives solely around Christ, using these schismatic codifications as foundations for liberatory politics misses the mark and once again sidesteps the radical call of the gospel. Gay people, I will argue, offer new and exciting methods of understanding sexuality and organizing sociosexual life, methods that could be helpful models for the church in its quest for a more faithful way of life. Chapter 4 challenges the hegemonic discourse that requires gay people to imitate the nuclear family, and points out the value of certain alternative lifestyles for Christian community.

Chapter 5 challenges the coherency of the new ecclesial category "nonpracticing homosexual" by asking what—other than their practices—makes homosexuals different from heterosexuals. Those who theorize an essential difference between the two, I suggest, unnecessarily divide the Body of Christ. Civil rights activists in the church of the 1950s understood the importance of unifying blacks and whites within the church; as the head of the National Council of Churches Will D. Campbell preached in 1956: "By God's grace we are no longer Negro or white . . . but we are a part of a community which asks only one question that has to do with redemption, not color."[1] It is time that we recognize that the categories of "gay" and "straight" unnecessarily rend the church and need to be transcended. The old ways of understanding gender and sexuality are no longer adequate. We are in the middle of forging new ways. Like the civil rights workers before us, our central questions ought to do not with preference but with redemption; we should be asking not whether gay people should be allowed to fit in, but rather which historically gay practices can help renew and heal the church today.

We have inherited a world in which sex itself is a conflicted enterprise. It is no longer (if it ever was) an activity used solely as a means of reproducing the species.[2] Yet few think of sex as simply a way to obtain pleasure and enjoyment. In some ways, we are told that sex is the *only* way that each of us can truly be known and defined, that we aren't truly "coupled" with another unless we are sexually active with that person. In other conversations (especially those associated with the sexual revolution), indiscriminate sex becomes the route by which we mark our liberation. As Christians, we are charged with the difficult task of sorting out which constructions of sexual activities belong in the new creation as outlined for us by Christ, and which concepts must be rejected. This is the work of this book: to examine various attitudes toward and understandings of sexuality in order to construct a coherent, Christian-based system of sexual ethics.

The recent attention given to women's and gay liberation in our culture gives us several new perspectives on sexual ethics. In many ways, the very concept of "sexual ethics" arises only out of a set of social events like the women's movement; before these, the only religious thinkers who systematically addressed sexuality were Roman Catholic—and then it was largely to condemn intercourse outside of reproduction. Before the contemporary women's movement, many Catholic moral theologians—as well as many of the silent Protestant Christian ethicists—did not see women as significant sexual subjects. Sex, for most people, was composed of the right ordering of male desire and female response. No "ethics" were necessary as long as everyone agreed that one person's (the male's) desires took precedence, that one person (the male) was in charge. Only when it was accepted that God cares as much about women's agency and sexuality as about men's could the conditions for a conversation called "sexual ethics" arise.

The recent increase in visibility of gays, lesbians, and bisexuals, both in the church and in society as a whole, helps to further solidify this discourse of sexual ethics. It is no longer possible for anyone to assume that sex occurs only between married heterosexuals who "do it" to have babies. Given this shift, we are forced to come up with some ideas about why any of us "do it." And if we reject the Christian Right's assertion that all homosexual sex is bad and most married, heterosexual sex is good, it becomes important for us to define what makes some sex acceptable and other sex unethical. If the line between moral sex and immoral sex is not based on the gender of the people involved, on what basis will we judge right from wrong? Based once again on the idea that sex and spirituality ought to be intricately interwoven, this book's final chapter proposes a coherent sexual ethic for Christians. Based on biblical narratives about hospitality, it suggests that sex is ethical when it opens God's world to others.

This book is written for those of us who hear and desire to respond faithfully to the call of the living God. It is for those of us who have not yet given up on the institutional church. It is for those of us who believe that Christ's story—as it defeats death and isolation—is the most radical narrative ever told. It is for those of us who believe that the spirit of God still dwells in our communities. While I focus here on mainline Protestantism, I hope the arguments will be extended and translated into other settings such as Catholicism and black churches. Moreover, I do not mean to suggest that more progressive organizations and denominations such as Metropolitan Community Church and Quakers have not done a wonderful job bringing sexuality to the forefront of their Christian communities. They have. What I offer here is an argument meant to persuade all Christians of the importance of these issues.

However, I do not mean to suggest that the church, especially in its current state, can offer clear thinking to the secular world regarding issues of gender equity, homosexuality, or sexual ethics. In fact the opposite is true; our churches are divided, unclear, and often extremely oppressive in relation to these issues. I do mean to suggest that if we Christians took our historical commitment to community as seriously as many of our ancestors did, we could understand sex and gender in a whole new, more faithful light, and act accordingly.

As I wrote and thought about these materials, I found that my own relationship to them was troubled. As I attempted to delineate the theological world of conservative Christians and to take their claims seriously, I continued to be dismayed and frightened by the Right's political convictions. But every once in a while, I found a grain of truth embedded in their rhetoric, a statement about God's love, forgiveness, or the workings of the spirit, an idea that our lives were made possible totally and completely by God. While my own life has been overwhelmingly influenced by the mainline Protestantism of which I am now a part and the socially conscious Catholicism of my youth, the religious expressions and commitment of the Right were deeply attractive to me in some ways. Sometimes it was hard to separate their legitimate and faithful assertions about God from their corrupt and hateful opinions about women and gays.

I was often equally uncomfortable with the politics of mainline Christianity today. There, I found theologians, ethicists, and public thinkers who were happy to accept gay people, as long as they could look, act, and pass as straight. I was surprised to find that most mainliners were quite content with the constitution of their churches and understood their Christian duty to be synonymous with tolerance. Allowing strangers (such as blacks and gays) into your church (although not necessarily into your home) was, they believed, the central message of the gospel; learning to "get along" would win them salvation. I rarely, if ever, saw hope for radical spiritual renewal in the writings and worship of today's mainline denominations. I believe that the secular Left as a whole shies away from discussing or thinking about life's meaning, largely because such territory has been held for so long by religious conservatives. Because most mainline Christians would much rather be mistaken for secular liberals than for religious conservatives, they seem to shy away from too much fervor for or discussion about God as well.

Hence, the second half of this book attempts to revive the political struggles in the mainline church, specifically around issues of sexuality. Raised by parents and teachers deeply involved in socially progressive Christianity, I learned that my faith had consequences wider than simple acceptance of difference. I learned that I had responsibilities to the poor, oppressed, and suffering, I learned that—as Christians—we are all part of one another. At the end of my college years I discovered my own sexual preference and realized that the struggle for justice to which Christ calls us could and should be extended to my own sexual orientation, as well as to my womanhood (which I had somehow overlooked before that point as well). Thus, feminism and gay liberation became, for me, part of that larger project of Christian social action. Although Christians have never accepted the struggles for "women's lib" and "gay rights" as full-fledged social issues, this book stands as an invitation to all those who struggle for the gospel vision to take these issues more seriously.

It is my hope and deepest desire that the community-based sexual ethic I set forth can be heard not only by liberation-oriented Christians but by conservative evangelicals, that it can unite people on both sides of the divide. I hope it will bridge another gap as well: that between religion and politics. My own religious experiences have taught me that to love God means to struggle for justice, that the two cannot and ought not to be separated. In the reality of this broken world, however, most often I find myself forced to separate the two aspects of my commitment from each other, to do my political work over here, my religious work over there. I long for a community that can speak about the moral and political nature of sexuality and about the God who gives us life—in the same conversation. What follows is in many ways an attempt to unite all Christians in the common project of discerning God's call for us today.

While the history and background in chapter 1 sketch some basic differences between the Christian Right and mainline Christianity, the entire book attempts to dig deeper into the social and theological mind-sets of the two groups. Chapter 1 records the differences between their organizing strategies, campaign initiatives, and political successes; the rest of the book follows the hunch that these observable differences have much to do with attitudes toward sex, gender, homosexuality, and subsequent relationship with God. Thus, chapters 2 and 3 examine the ideology of family values and argue that in the rhetoric of the Christian Right, sexism and homophobia are inextricably linked. The final three chapters help us think about how we might reconstruct a theological sexual ethic for the next century in a manner that takes both God and sex—and the relationship between them—seriously.

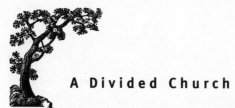

CHAPTER ONE

A Divided Church

The Political Landscape of Contemporary Christianity

> *One liberal straight churchman frankly told me that "too much emphasis" on abortion, sex education, and gay rights would burn too many "ecumenical bridges" between Christians. A reasonable and charitable position? Those "bridges" are built on our backs. Let them burn.*

Scott Tucker, *Fighting Words*

In a small northeastern town in 1970, a group of Roman Catholic nuns took a couple of busloads of Catholic high school students away for a weekend retreat. If the retreat had happened fifteen years earlier in 1955, the students would have been praying for homes in the suburbs with two-car garages and automatic dishwashers. If it had happened fifteen years later in 1985, the students would have been engaging in something called "values clarification," a new style of ethics which suggested that the social worth of any action or attitude could be understood quantitatively, (and hence, who ought to survive in the proverbial lifeboat became a simple mathematical problem). But it didn't. It happened in 1970, the culmination of the sixties, and the teens participated in workshops on the sin of war, the plight of the United Farm Workers, the injustice of the criminal justice system, the lack of adequate housing for the poor, the iniquity of capitalism, racism in American institutions, world hunger, and women's role in church and society. The students learned from that retreat that their faith in a loving God would require them to become earnestly involved in social action. Neither a rich prayer life nor worldly success nor even a personal code of ethics would fulfill their Christian obligation, for they were called to change the world.

The scene was replayed in many other high schools, colleges, churches, and religious institutions across America. Christians saw secular liberation movements such as civil rights and women's rights as possible ways to understand faithfulness in a turbulent, troubled age. Pope John XXIII encouraged all Christians to open the windows of their churches and welcome the spirit of renewal. In America, opening those windows most often meant extending Christian community to the poor and disenfranchised. It meant learning how to welcome women and blacks in positions of church leadership, and it meant helping congregations become integrated along racial and class lines. In many middle-class white churches of the 1970s, it was believed that renewal would only happen as churches opened their doors to people who, for one reason or another, had not quite fit in before.

This recent moment of political rejuvenation in the American church is as good a place as any to begin to understand the bifurcated and contentious nature of the church, particularly its understandings of sexuality and gender, at the turn of the twenty-first century. Sandwiched between desires for suburbia on the one hand and the institutionalization and objectification of the "situation ethics" movement on the other, pockets of Christians all over the country heard the gospel message in the late sixties and early seventies as a revolutionary claim about inclusivity, community, and social action. For them, the older patterns of life—in which white men from the middle or upper classes dominated their families, their local churches, and Christian thinking and writing itself—were no longer adequate. From every walk of life and from every political angle, Christians across America challenged hegemony, race and class privilege, and sexism; moreover, they spoke against a church that allowed and sanctioned oppression and injustice. New voices were welcomed as fresh authorities.

However, for Christians who were relatively happy with the status quo, these new liberation theologies and movements seemed excessive, ungrounded, and unnecessary. Before the sixties, churches were growing; the American family was stable and healthy; and a national consensus existed regarding the importance of church life. Although blacks, women, and gays were regularly excluded from the ranks of church leadership, it was, in the words of one commentator, a "time of peace and prosperity when people moved to the suburbs, bought Chevrolets, went to bed early, and repopulated the Churches."[1] Although not everyone had a voice in public discourse, those who did speak for the church could at least agree on what American Christianity stood for. Thus, what some of us saw as spiritual renewal and long-needed challenges to straight, white, male hegemony, others saw as the unnecessary disruption of stability and religious consensus. By the late 1970s, Christians had become severely divided over which ideology truly embodied the gospel message.

In his *Culture Wars*, James Davison Hunter describes the differences between these competing factions by distinguishing "orthodoxy," which he defines as "commitment to an external, definable, and transcendent authority which defines a consistent, unchangeable measure of value, purpose, goodness, and identity," from "progressivism," which embodied the "spirit of the modern age," and entailed a strong affiliation with contemporary life. While proponents of orthodoxy exhibit a strong belief in the transcendence of God and the continuing appropriateness of traditional ways of organizing life, progressives "continuously resymbolize religious authority" because they believe that "traditional faith must be reworked to conform to new circumstances and conditions."[2] Hunter argues that the differences between the orthodox and the progressives were rooted in their contrasting attitudes toward change; these competing ideas about change produced the struggle to define which direction America would take in the future. Whether America should welcome new and different forms of religious expression, or whether we should stick with the tried and true methods of our forefathers lies, Hunter argues, at the heart of the culture wars.

In his study of the conflicts between liberal and conservative Christians, *The Restructuring of American Religion*, Robert Wuthnow points out that these competing factions were no longer organized along denominational lines. Whereas Christians before the mid-1960s were members of either liberal denominations (such as United Church of Christ or the Episcopal Church) or conservative denominations (such as Southern Baptist Convention or the Assemblies of God), Christians after the mid-1960s expressed and demonstrated their faith in small, politically and socially oriented groups that transcended both denominational and theological affiliation. Wuthnow explains this shift by noting that the ideology of the fifties and sixties placed a high degree of importance on individualism and personal preference, an emphasis which, he claims, eventually allowed mainline Protestant Christians to drift away from denominational allegiance on political issues and encouraged them to move more freely among local churches and church organizations based on individual preference. Individuals thus participated in a broad spectrum of social and political issues—from abortion to war to civil rights—and the result, according to Wuthnow, was the rise of special interest groups on both the Left and the Right. Americans did not become more secularized during this period, but American religious life did become organized on axes other than denominations. Ignoring older allegiances, people began seeking local congregations that reflected their political convictions and joining special interest groups and Christian organizations designed to enhance rather than replace congregational life. Whereas prewar controversies found denominations disagreeing with each other on social and political issues, denominations today are filled with individuals on both sides of any issue. In today's political landscape, tension and disagreement exist within each American mainline denomination rather than between them; as Wuthnow states, "The great divide between liberal and conservative cuts directly through the middle of many established denominations."[3] Thus, the differences between liberal and conservative Christians cannot be defined solely on the basis of denominational affiliation, but must be determined by other social, political, and theological factors.

Admittedly, without the firm rooting of denominational affiliation and with only the vague notion of "attitudes toward change" to go on, it is difficult to give a solid definition of the competing factions in Christian politics today. The contemporary cleft—for reasons I will discuss more fully—does not neatly fall out along fundamentalist versus modernist lines. Because conservatives today are quite different from (and enormously more sophisticated than) their fundamentalist ancestors, and because today's Christian progressives are equally distinct from their modernist forebears, the political landscape of our churches today warrants a more local and detailed map. In the following section, I offer one analysis of their differences, especially as they relate to sexuality and gender.

The influence of the "new" Christian Right in setting the agenda for national Christian politics cannot be overestimated. This movement began with the rise of four conservative organizations in the late 1970s. Between December 1978 and December 1979, the National Christian Action Coalition (NCAC), the Religious Roundtable, the Christian Voice, and the Moral Majority all opened offices in Washington, D.C., and jockeyed into position for the important 1980 election. Although Jimmy Carter had been elected the first born-again Christian president in 1976, he was too liberal and welcoming of change for many conservatives; his pro-choice position on abortion in particular made him suspect to the growing coalition of Christians who had demonized the sexual revolution. These new conservative organizations opened Washington offices to work for the election of Ronald Reagan because they believed that he could redirect the spirit of the country and help them in their quest for a more "traditional" America. NCAC, for example, had first formed in 1978 to fight Internal Revenue Service attempts to revoke the tax-exempt status of schools that were discriminating on the basis of race. NCAC president Bob Billings hoped that Reagan's election would curtail this liberal, integrationist trend by limiting the power of the IRS. The NCAC produced a newsletter for fundamentalist churches that outlined Christian reasons why Reagan should be elected. Similarly, the Religious Roundtable was formed primarily to recruit fundamentalist ministers into politics with the expectation that they would bring their congregations with them. Reagan was the keynote speaker of their widely attended 1980 conference "A National Affairs Briefing." The Christian Voice functioned primarily as a lobby group against gay rights (especially in California), and in 1980 produced its first "report card" on political candidates, which highlighted gay issues. Finally, the Moral Majority raised $11 million before 1980, and spent much of it lobbying for Reagan and to get key social issues placed on the congressional agenda. These groups brought a new kind of verve to Christian politics, and new ways to integrate conservative Christians into the Republican party. Soon after Reagan's election, Republican leaders in turn began to encourage preacher-politicians such as Jerry Falwell to enter the political arena. These Christians brought with them both votes and funding, as well as the resources of a multitude of nascent local political organizations. In return for this support, Republican Party leaders met regularly with these ministers and, in many cases, took seriously their concerns regarding the immoral attitudes that had taken over America.

By the end of Reagan's first term in office, these new Christian activists could look back on many accomplishments as well as some major losses. They had registered a massive number of voters (Falwell claimed that his ministry alone registered over two million voters for the 1984 campaign);[4] had placed conservative social issues such as school prayer, abortion, and aid to the Nicaraguan Contras on the congressional agenda; and had established innumerable grassroots organizations from which both voters and local candidates could be recruited. Despite these successes, however, the Right had yet to win any major initiative on the national level. Moreover, energies and funding sources for work in Washington were fading; all four of the original organizations had left Washington by 1984, and each closed its door permanently by the end of 1986. To survive in politics, the movement needed a new style of organizing that would both utilize and simultaneously replenish the resources of local constituencies.

There emerged a new group of conservative leaders who realized that certain strategic changes needed to be made. Most prominent among these new leaders was Paul Weyrich, who quickly coined the phrase "cultural conservative" to indicate

that conservatism transcended not only fundamentalism, but Christianity altogether, and could include Jews and secularists. This change made the agenda of the
new Christian Right more palatable to many other conservatives in America. These
new leaders also realized that the political agendas adopted by the first wave of religious conservatives were often too remote for many Americans; abortion and
Contra aid had little impact on the lives of most conservative voters. Issues such as
what was being taught in local public schools and whether gay people should be
allowed to teach, marry, or hold office, on the other hand, held the interest of many
more conservative Americans. Instead of national campaigns and congressional
lobbying, the new leaders focused the discussion on local and state issues, including school board elections and gay rights referenda. Finally, as a result of the
various televangelist scandals, the new style of politics promulgated by conservative leaders took the focus off of one or two prominent leaders and put it on local leaders. As Concerned Women of America (CWA) founder Beverly LaHaye comments, "Jerry was the Moral Majority for the most part. He spoke and that was
it. CWA is very different from that. We have state leaders, state chapters, steer-
ing committee, almost a thousand prayer action chapters—an army of people out
there working on local and state issues. CWA may not get as much press attention,
but I'm not sure I miss it. Leave us alone. Let us get the job done."[5] Hence, the leadership of conservative Christianity in this second wave was spread among many
people.

Pat Robertson's campaign for the 1988 Republican presidential nomination was the
Christian Right's last attempt at involvement in presidential politics. Although the
campaign failed to bring him the nomination, it continued to shore up evangelical
support for conservative party politics.[6] The central message of the Robertson campaign seemed to be not that Robertson himself ought to be elected but rather that
all Christians should be involved in American politics, a message that continued to
have an effect on conservative Christians long after this particular nomination was
lost. After the 1988 campaign failed, Pat Robertson quickly established the Christian Coalition, an organization that, as Robertson claims, "hopes to mobilize Christians—one precinct at a time, one community at a time—until once again we are the
head and not the tail, and at the top rather than the bottom of our political system."[7] In founding the Christian Coalition, Robertson thus made a deliberate decision to join with other conservative organizers in moving from national politics to
local, grassroots elections. As Ralph Reed, the executive director of the Christian Co-

alition, states, "We tried to change Washington [in 1988] when we should have been focusing on the states. . . . The real battles of concern to Christians are in the neighborhoods, school boards, city councils and state legislatures."[8]

To achieve these positions of power, conservative Christians initially ran in low visibility campaigns.[9] As Reed states it, the Christian Right waged a "stealth war, under the cover of night," where "every moment you disguise your position because the minute you stick your head up, you can be shot."[10] Jay Grimstead, the director of the Republican coordinating council in California, describes this philosophy as follows: "The county and the liberals and the media won't know it until [newly elected officials] take their seats and prove themselves to be what you would call Christian-right people."[11] The success of flying below radar is patent; while the Left celebrated the fact that the Christian Right had failed to reelect George Bush in 1992, the Christian right could count many other successes. More than 1,000 Christians directly sponsored by Robertson's Christian Coalition or endorsed by the conservative Christian network ran for office in 1992 across the country; by many estimates, over half of them won. Conservative leader Tim LaHaye claimed that "The Lord is going to give us this nation back one precinct at a time, one neighborhood at a time, and one state at a time. We're not going to win it all at once with some kind of millennial rush at the White House."[12]

One of the major features that distinguished the contemporary Christian Right from its turn-of-the-century fundamentalist counterparts was the new generation's aggressive use of television for political as well as evangelizing purposes. While the older fundamentalism was often narrow, negative, and separatist, the newer conservative Christianity, especially from 1980 to 1988, sought a much wider membership by using television to reach a larger audience. Although communications scholars ardently debate the constitution and size of the televangelist viewing audience, as well as the impact that televangelist programming had on those viewers, most agree that aggressive use of this technology differentiated the new Christian Right from its precursors. As early as 1981, authors Jeffrey Hadden and Charles Swann argued that televangelism had the potential to become a major force in shaping American culture. Recognizing that every modern social movement has utilized mass media, Hadden and Swann suggested that American religion had undergone an important transformation through its adoption of modern communications.[13] Although the nature and value of this transformation was unclear, a

significant part of the new Christian Right's success can be attributed to their innovative and foreceful use of the technology.

Even several scandals involving televangelists helped shore up the identity of conservative Christianity. Between 1986 and 1988, Oral Roberts claimed that God
would kill him if Americans didn't send him $8 million, Jimmy Swaggart was in-
volved in a relatively minor sex scandal, and Jim and Tammy Bakker were implicated
in much larger sex and embezzlement scandals. At the time, many critics saw these
developments as the downfall of conservative Christianity, but I suggest that they
in fact helped to police the boundaries of conservative membership. The scandals
reminded the evangelists' followers that sin could erupt at any moment into the
lives of clean-living Christians; thus the Right needed to define even more clearly
what a "Christian" was and how a "Christian" lived, so that those who did not satisfy these definitions could be cast out. The circle of conservative Christianity could
include those like Swaggart who had repented of their sins, but not those who per-
sisted in what the Right saw as unclean living. While it might have *former* sinners,
former adulterers, *former* homosexuals, *former* militant feminists in its ranks, the
Right contained none of these undesirable elements who still practiced their sins;
its self-definition was based on these specific claims to moral high ground. Consequently, even though contemporary conservative religion invited a much wider circle of membership through television, it also used the medium to constantly and
narrowly define and redefine the Christian life.

Conservative Christians did not limit their political organizing tactics to television.
Indeed, as the second generation of leaders emphasized local issues and local campaigns, they turned to more conventional church-based methods to increase voter
turnout and commitment. Radio, mass mailings, rallies, book and sound recordings
sales, telephone, leafleting, and personal contacts as well as local television helped
get their candidates elected. Across the nation, local volunteers collected names
from church directories for mailings and telephone banks, conducted voter registra-
tion drives at churches, and distributed thousands of flyers in church parking lots on
Sunday. As one reporter put it, "Conservative Christians have moved beyond using
television as their principal tool to organizing local communities in ways that by-
pass mainstream media and thus escape scrutiny. [National broadcasts] should be
understood less as a mechanism for the conversion of a mass public audience and
more as a reinforcement for a growing army of stealth-trained ground troops."[14]

These "stealth-trained troops" are radically different from their turn-of-the-century fundamentalist ancestors, not only in their more sophisticated use of media, but also because they were born into or lived through the turbulent years of Vietnam and the civil rights and women's movements. Indeed it was precisely their strong reaction to and organization against the liberation movements—particularly sexual liberation movements—of the sixties that politicized this new group of Christian activists. In my view, the Christian Right emerged as a dominant and influential phenomenon in the late twentieth century not because it brought religion into contemporary American living rooms, but rather because it encouraged and gave voice to resistance to change in various areas of sexuality, integrating that resistance with traditional religious practices, conservative attitudes, and backlash politics.

As a result of the wider political struggles for women's rights, gay rights, and sexual freedom, the "family" (and by this, as we shall see, these Christians mean a particular kind of family) became the overriding issue for the Christian Right, subsuming in its fold such topics as the teaching of evolution, prayer in schools, abortion, traditional roles for women, sex, drugs, pornography, and homosexuality. As Grant Wacker comments,

> *In the perspective of the Evangelical Right, the arbiters of contemporary culture who pose the most deadly threat to Christian Civilization are not media folk, nor educators, but the enemies of the traditional patriarchal, nuclear family. What the historian sees as a cluster of closely related cultural changes, the Evangelical Right experiences as a finely tuned conspiracy, coordinated by a master blueprint of international scope. To the members of the Evangelical Right, the* Attack on the Family, *as James Robison describes it, or* The Battle for the Family, *as Tim LaHaye describes it, is so perfectly orchestrated it could not be anything except the handiwork of the Antichrist. The leaders of the movement consider the general loosening of sexual restraints the most conspicuous manifestation of the Antichrist's determination to destroy the family.*[15]

As I will demonstrate in the next two chapters, the Christian Right works hard to show, theologically, that women belong at home, out of the competitive public sphere. Ideologies that challenge this arrangement, such as the contemporary feminist movement, are understood as anathema. For similar reasons, the social movement of the last two decades that has brought homosexuality into the public eye is seen as threatening not only because homosexuality is more visible than it was before 1960, but also because it threatens the Right's "traditional" family formula. Both the women's movement and the gay liberation movement challenge older, established constructions of gender differentiation; the Christian Right's popularity rests on the fact that it offers a theologically sanctioned voice for conservative resistance to newer models of family living.

While some commentators suggest that the Christian Right reached its peak membership in the mid-1980s and has been decreasing in power since,[16] most see evidence to the opposite. Across the country, the Christian Right has won seats in state assemblies, city councils, zoning commissions, and school boards. Most of these campaigns were based on a broad appeal to family values. The bills and legislation proposed and often passed by these conservatives are consistently opposed to homosexuality. In fact, many bills pitch the civil rights of ethnic and racial minorities against the rights of gay and lesbian people; thus, even when a socially progressive bill appears among conservatives, it does so usually at the expense of gays, lesbians, and bisexuals. In one New York City school board meeting, to take just one example, conservative Christians advocated the agendas of ethnic and racial interest groups, but did so at the expense of lesbian and gay concerns. As Mary Cummins, a longtime affiliate of the Christian Right and school board member stated, "I will not demean our legitimate minorities, such as blacks, Hispanics and Asians, by lumping them together with homosexuals in the curriculum."[17]

On the state level as well, a number of proposals have been introduced that challenge the civil rights of gay people. In Colorado, officials elected in 1992 and associated with the Christian Right were able to pass Amendment 2, which cut back the basic constitutional protection of gay people. These Christians argued that "homosexuals were wealthy playboys seeking not equal rights but 'special rights' at the expense of working people." After two years in court, judges struck down the measure; this occurred, however, just one month before the November 8, 1994, election which, in most Colorado locales, the Christian Right won by a landslide. Five of seven Christian candidates for state assembly were elected, setting the stage for an avalanche of new, socially conservative legislation. Moreover, the three open slots on the Colorado State Board of Education were also filled by conservative Christians. Similarly, although Oregon's 1992 Measure 9—which stated that homosexuality was abnormal, wrong, unnatural, and perverse—was defeated in a state referendum 57 percent to 43 percent, a more mildly worded version was introduced again in 1994. This Measure 13 was also defeated, but by a less-than-1-percent margin. Conservatives in Idaho in 1994 sponsored Proposition 1 with the stated goals of banning gay rights ordinances, preventing teachers from discussing homosexuality, and limiting library books to adults only; this legislation was also defeated by a less-than-1-percent margin.[18] Even though these particular state referenda banning the legal rights of gay people have all failed or been overturned, with them the Christian Right has set a political tone in which more and more Americans feel that sexism and homophobia are acceptable political options.

The Christian Right candidates who ran at the local level fared better than proposed legislation. By most estimates, 60 percent of the 600 conservative Christian candidates running from coast to coast were elected in 1994, up from 40 percent just two years earlier.[19] Clear Republican victories in both the House and Senate were in large part due to conservative Christian involvement. Born-again Christian David Beasley—whose campaign was largely funded by the Christian Coalition—won the South Carolina gubernatorial race. And even though Oliver North lost his Senate race in Virginia, his "Pray AND Vote" campaign (which included the slogan "Homophobia Never Killed Anyone") organized a massive number of Christian voters. Republican candidates in 1994 issued a clear statement of policy goals and priorities in the Contract with America, a fiscally oriented program designed to strengthen the traditional nuclear family, and to punish single and working mothers with welfare cuts and increased taxes. The Christian Coalition alone donated $1 million to promote the campaign at local levels. As one conservative commentator stated, "In exchange for their support of the Contract with America, religious conservatives are hoping for more pro-family legislation including conservative stands on limiting abortion; permitting a constitutional amendment on public school prayer; and curtailing the homosexual rights movement."[20] Given these developments, it seems clear that, even though leaders like Jerry Falwell no longer hold the nation's rapt attention, the Christian Right is far from defunct. Indeed, it comprises a formidable strength in the political landscape of American Christianity. And even though part of its enormous success comes from its innovative use of new technologies, the Right hammers home the ideology that the norms and characteristics of what it means to be an American Christian can best be found in "the way things used to be."

On the other side of the divide stands liberal Christianity, a phenomenon that is more fragmented than conservatism and consequently more difficult to discuss. Liberal Christians in America today are the direct product of the liberation movements of the sixties. Many of the people populating our mainline churches today are the very same people who watched footage from Vietnam with horror, who marched for civil rights or against the war, who shared in the flickers of hope that things, perhaps, could be better. These were the people who heard the gospel proclaimed in Acts 2:17: "I will pour out my Spirit upon all flesh, and your sons and your daughters shall prophesy, and your young men shall see visions, and your old men shall dream dreams," and knew that they were called by God to build a better world. Today, these are the people who sit in the pews of our mainline churches and occasionally remember that they once thought they could change the world, even though they may be less sure about what a better world might look like.

According to both Hunter and Wuthnow, liberal Christianity is marked by its persistent desire for tolerance. As Hunter describes it, "First and foremost among the shared beliefs [of liberals] is a celebration of diversity and respect for the beliefs of others."[21] Similarly, from Wuthnow's perspective, liberal ideology is one that enables the growth of a multitude of special interest groups within the church. In social situations where diversity is celebrated, marks of difference—age, gender, race— are held up and honored. These are the Christians that are proud of the black families that hold membership in their congregations, that are happy to receive or call a woman pastor, that may even permit a gay couple to hold a commitment ceremony in their church. These are the people who fundamentally believe that it is wrong to judge others on the basis of race, ethnicity, creed, gender, or sexual preference. But the concrete vision of a better future prominent in the 1960s has generally faded into the idea that building a better world largely entails being more tolerant of each other's differences. Hence, these people construct their politics along the line of pluralism, believing that by accepting those who are unlike them, change will naturally follow. By opening their churches and businesses and social clubs to "others," they believe they are being faithful to the heart of the gospel message.

Thus, while the Christian Right preaches a gospel of exclusion, liberal mainline Christians often argue for an agenda of tolerance. This agenda is disseminated not by sophisticated media blitzes, but rather by the close correlation between liberal mainline Christianity and standard, middle-class American life. From the perspective of liberal Christians, tolerance is part and parcel of what it means to be both Christian and American. While many participants in conservative Christianity view themselves as separate from this strand of American ideology, most liberal Christians understand tolerance and pluralism to be essential.

Some liberal Christians have avoided the narrower liberalism associated with plu-ralism in favor of more radical versions that associate Christianity with positive goals for social change. These Christians hear the gospel as a call to question these seemingly inherent differences between black and white, rich and poor, propertied and homeless. The lives and works of Dorothy Day, Martin Luther King, Cesar Cha-vez, Oscar Romero, and Daniel Berrigan stand as historical models for a Christianity that will not tolerate injustice, oppression, poverty, and discrimination. In many sit-uations, local churches, denominations, and other voluntary associations and gov-erning ecclesial bodies take prophetic stands to change the world.[22] Indeed, in America today, thousands of Christians are responding to the message of Christ in rather radical formats; Jim Wallis astutely captures the vision and faith that lie be-hind these communities:

> Over the past few decades, a spiritually based activism has become visible in reli-gious efforts to end the threat of nuclear war, in congregations providing sanctu-ary to Central American refugees or building new houses for the homeless, in the creation of dynamic church-based coalitions for community organizing, and in religious efforts to renew creation. In both cities and rural areas across the coun-try, the number of spiritually based ventures and coalitions to heal and rebuild local communities is beyond counting. New faith communities have emerged in urban ministry centers, homeless shelters, and soup kitchens; in street protests and jail cells; on racial and ecological battlegrounds; and in diverse experiments in community and spiritual renewal. This new prophetic spirituality . . . draws evangelicals with a compassionate heart and social conscience. It brings together mainline Protestants who desire spiritual revival and justice. It invites Catholics who seek a spirituality for social change. It attracts those who, long alienated from established religion, are hungry for a personal and communal spirituality to undergird their struggle to live more justly.[23]

And yet, homophobia and gender oppression rarely evoke the same kind of concern on the Christian Left—and almost never the support of mainline institutions—as do those issues not associated with sexuality.[24] Indeed, Christians involved in the struggles against racism, classism, and war often even agree with their conserva-tive counterparts in their assertion that homosexuality is immoral and incommen-surate with the Christian paradigm. In some ways, the very structure of spirituality underpinning these social movements depends directly on certain configurations of gender and sexuality, a certain way of putting male and female together to achieve relationship with God. It is often the case that leftist Christians are able to fight for racial and class liberation because they have a "stable, intact family" at home to support them emotionally, physically, and spiritually. The goodness of this family—where mom stays home to raise the kids and dad goes out to the cold world by day and returns by night to his "haven in a heartless world"—is, for them, the ground that cannot be questioned.

Liberal Christianity's lack of coherence on positions about women and sexuality has allowed the Right's rhetoric to fill the public void. Indeed, the Right has begun to control the media-generated, public image of the church, so much so that Christianity is now sometimes equated with conservative politics in the minds of many secular Americans. In order to begin to think more clearly about gender and homosexuality in the frame of Christian ethics, we first need to examine the Right's theology more closely. Only by investigating the theological logic of conservative Christianity can we begin to understand why it is so powerful, deep-seated, and persuasive. And only after we understand the appeal of conservative Christianity can we construct a more progressive and faithful ethic for the Left.

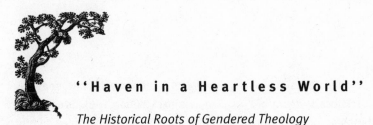

CHAPTER TWO

"Haven in a Heartless World"

The Historical Roots of Gendered Theology

*When I have been out having a long, hard day, often in a hostile environment,
it is great to walk into my home, to close the front door, and to know that inside
the home there is a wife who loves me. Home is a haven to which I run from the
troubles of this world.*

Jerry Falwell, *The Old Time Gospel Hour*

Imagine for a moment that you are a young woman in America in 1820. Your husband is a farmer and you live in one of the land grant territories of the Midwest. You know the role of farmer's wife well, because your mother and virtually all the women you know lived, worked, and died farming. You will toil in the fields alongside your husband, making sure that the corn or the wheat has what it needs to grow. You will cook the food, mend and wash the clothes, clean the house, perhaps even teach the children to read and write; your husband will attend to these tasks or others and together you will provide daily sustenance for you and your children. You believe that life will go on like this forever.

But one day your husband comes home from town with a penny paper advertisement announcing employment opportunities at a soon-to-be-built nearby factory. Your husband could make more money in a month of hauling lumber or cutting cloth or pouring steel than he could in a year of farming, and he's eager to try. He wants to build a better life for you and the kids, he says. So next fall he goes off to town and you plant only a kitchen garden, just enough for your small but growing family, and you set about the business of waiting for him to return. He likes the work, and little by little you sell the farm and maybe even move closer to town so your husband doesn't have so far to travel on Friday nights. Instead of staying at home to learn their lessons, the kids go to the little red schoolhouse which is only a mile away. Life is easier on you now with only the cooking, cleaning, and household chores to keep up with.

Oddly enough, however, you're more and more tired. In increments that are almost too small to notice, your family's expectations of you change. They are no longer satisfied with the same kettle of stew for two or three dinners; they have to have different foods every night and even different foods at the same meal. Nobody has just two sets of clothes anymore, and your family is no exception. The kids need new pants and shirts and dresses and shoes all the time, and different ones still for church on Sunday. Your husband makes enough money to buy some of the clothes from the store in town, but keeping them all clean is a real challenge. When you lived back on the farm, your kids took a bath once a week; now the older ones think they need to bathe daily so the other kids at school won't make fun of them. A little dirt in the house is embarrassing, they say, and they can't bring their friends over to such a mess. Why can't you clean more? What else do you have to do? they want to know. Without such amenities as indoor plumbing, electricity, or a cook stove (none of which was available then), these demands seem overwhelming. Perhaps the most disturbing changes are the ones that are expected of your own body. Your old, homemade farm dresses just won't do, your husband says. He's making enough money that you should be dressing better; showing you off is part of the way he shows the people in town how successful he is. He brings you new clothes for the church social, maybe even a little makeup and perfume, but suddenly getting dressed becomes yet another chore in your growing list of household jobs. The penny papers call women like you "housewives," and you realize that that is precisely what you've become.

You've always enjoyed going to church and reading the Bible, and both of these things become even more important to you during this time of change. The other women at church understand how hard these adjustments are, and they help you think about your new life as part of God's plan, indeed, as a way to help your children and your husband relate to God more consistently. You and the other women at church begin to understand that you have been freed from all that farmwork precisely to make certain that the Christian message is alive in your home. Reading stories of women in the Bible from this new perspective, you now see that the kind of life you're living is in fact what God had planned all along. When you discuss your daughter's upcoming marriage with her, you don't tell her about your mother's farm life, or the life you had working alongside your husband in the fields. Rather, you talk to her about her role as a young Christian wife.

The history that explains these changes in gender roles and domestic life sheds a great deal of light on the current political struggles surrounding gender and Christianity. Before industrialization, it was virtually impossible to live outside some sort of family or community, because the number of tasks needed to reproduce daily life were more than one person alone could handle. In most homes throughout the six-teenth and seventeenth centuries, everything from soap to jam, from firewood to meat was produced within the family unit. The family, then, was not only a place for the bearing and raising of children; it was also a unit for the production of the food and objects necessary for survival. The economic sphere was located within the home, not outside it.

The Industrial Revolution changed this. Almost overnight, it became quite possible for anyone—man or woman—to move into towns, to work in factories, and to live alone. As Linda Nicholson writes, "A market economy based on wages and payment for factory-produced goods undermined the necessity of the family as a means of survival, at least for adults able to obtain incomes of a certain size."[1] The economic base moved from the family to the "public sphere," that is, to the world of business and commerce, and the family was cordoned off into private space. And the private space of family, economically speaking, was no longer essential.[2]

If social life were organized on economics alone, the very idea of family might have dwindled with the onslaught of industry. It didn't, however, because a powerful, new logic that entered American life compelled individuals to continue to configure themselves inside families, even though such configurations were economically un-necessary. This new ideology organized people into kinship units by reconstructing the roles and attributes attached to each gender. Over the course of the nineteenth century, the daily responsibilities and social characteristics of men and women in America changed dramatically. In the new logic of gender, men became associated with competition, politics, business, and paid labor; women with religion, home, and family. Contemporary historians labeled this phenomenon "separate spheres," a metaphor that attempts to capture the idea that one sphere alone does not repre-sent a well-rounded life and that, in the ideology of the day, men and women need each other for complete and successful living.

It is important to note at the outset that the ideology of separate spheres existed largely among middle- and upper-class white women of the mid-nineteenth century. As many historians of women have pointed out, black women, ethnic women, and women of the lower classes were not relegated to the home or private sphere during industrialization; indeed, they continued to work outside the home in factory sweatshops as well as in positions of domestic labor. By focusing on those women who had the privilege of staying home, I do not mean to imply that these middle-

and upper-class women represented all women's experiences in nineteenth cen-tury. Rather, I focus on the doctrine of separate spheres because in my research I found that the rhetoric and ideology of the contemporary Christian Right most closely resembles that of the Cult of Domesticity associated with separate spheres.[3]

In the logic of separate spheres, the women's sphere of home and family increas-ingly came to be thought of as the sole refuge from outside life, the "haven in a heartless world." Although it appeared that women had fewer responsibilities and less work, expectations about the function and role of home and family in fact rose dramatically during this period. Indeed, the definition of home as the woman's sphere was accompanied by ideological changes about household life itself.[4] Tech-nologies enabled houses and children to be neater, more intricate, more present-able, attributes that signified a family's success in the new order. Thus, although every adult person—in theory—could have survived independently on his or her own wages, the logic of the day dictated that every man needed a woman to guaran-tee honor, order, and morality in his household. Furthermore, as William Chafe writes, "A wife who did not work outside the home constituted a badge of having achieved middle-class status."[5] Of course, keeping women at home and out of the public sphere also reduced the labor pool and thereby allowed men more opportu-nity for success. Together, the male and female gender roles functioned to produce a family that would help men succeed in the world of business and industry while simultaneously signifying that success.

The ideological shifts that reconfigured family life were reinforced by ideas on the nature of women that circulated in the popular literature of the day.[6] From pulp fic-tion to magazine sequels, from popular psychology to preaching, women were portrayed as more emotional, kinder, purer, and more pious than men. In her groundbreaking 1966 essay "The Cult of True Womanhood," historian Barbara Wel-ter claimed that women were seen as the moral leaders of the new, industrialized world, possessing the virtues of piety, purity, and submissiveness.[7] Because women were seen as morally and spiritually superior to men, women were better suited to the tasks of raising good citizens and providing a clean home. A cleaner home and purer children, it was believed, would eventually lead to a stronger nation.

While Welter herself saw the Cult of True Womanhood, or the Cult of Domesticity as confining for women—her use of the word *cult* was meant to be derogatory—other historians saw in the systematic separation of spheres opportunities for women to make connections, to advance female-centered agendas, and to exert control. For some, control of the home meant control of reproduction, which eventually led to liberation. As families moved closer to towns and away from farms, fewer children were needed or wanted; thus, in gaining control of their fertility, women were one step closer to suffrage and to the political activism associated with later birth control movements.[8] Other historians argued that the Cult of Domesticity gave nineteenth-century women the tools to think about themselves as women. While women gathered at church socials to discuss their families and other domestic issues, they were also developing, according to Nancy Cott, "women's perception of 'womanhood,'" a perception that was a necessary precondition to feminism.[9] By encouraging women to see themselves as a separate group, with different interests, needs and rights, domesticity paved the way for feminism. Indeed, the separation of spheres allowed women to create, as Carroll Smith-Rosenberg articulates it, "a female world of love and ritual in which men made but a shadowy appearance."[10] The relative merit of the separation of spheres are still contested among many historians and feminist theorists today.[11]

It cannot be emphasized too strongly that the ideology that described women as pure and passionless extended only to white, middle-class women. By and large, black women were conversely viewed as sexually insatiable. Although being caught up in the Cult of Domesticity was limiting for many white women, these ideas protected them from the rape and sexual abuse regularly imposed on black women.[12] This focus on white women in the nineteenth century is important because it gives us insight into the development and logic of gender among advocates of the contemporary Christian Right. Only by studying the cultural, domestic, and religious antecedents of conservative Christians today can we understand their positions in today's political environment.[13]

Religion played a twofold role in the development and maintenance of the ideology of women's sphere. First, as Cott and Smith-Rosenberg have shown, organized churches and denominational bodies were the first legitimate meeting places for women, and it was in church that women first learned to connect with each other. Religion was a powerful organizational force for the establishment of reform and benevolence movements, the creation of women's culture, and the necessary precursor to feminism. Most importantly, the church provided the aegis under which Christian women learned organizational skills and assumed positions of authority. Over the course of the nineteenth century, female church and voluntary organizations became involved in a long list of social struggles which began with temperance and abolition, and grew to include urban development, social welfare programs, social work, the settlement house movement, immigrant education, labor reform, and eventually, of course, suffrage. Many reform impulses of the nineteenth century found their leadership and their organizational and moral centers in church.

Second, religion played an ideological role in the development and maintenance of the Cult of Domesticity. During this period, women were seen not simply as better human beings, but also as better Christians than men. Here, morality and spirituality were deeply intertwined; a woman was better suited to raise the children, it was believed, because she was better at living and teaching the Christian faith. Women were thought to be more naturally equipped to receive and live the Christian message; women's meekness, imagination, sensitivity, and emotional nature made them, to nineteenth-century eyes, more Christlike.[14] As Christ brought redemption to the world through his suffering and patience, women could bring redemption to their own families by practicing the same virtues. As evangelist Billy Sunday was to articulate it fifty years later, "Jesus and women can save this old world. It remains with womanhood today to lift our social life to a higher plane."[15] Through a wife and mother's moral fiber and religious orientation, each family could directly participate in the redemption of Christ.[16]

These special attributes of women gave each nineteenth-century family a foolproof access and connection to God, and through this guarantee the structure of the family remained intact. That is, women were thought to be the point of contact between God and an entire family; in order to be ensured a place in the theological order, every person needed to be a member of a traditional family, with a mother at home to provide moral and spiritual instruction and maintenance. The nineteenth-century paradigm of separate spheres guaranteed relationship to God by placing everyone inside a family, and making one member of that family (the one most present and available) responsible for the spiritual life of every member.[17] Thus, while the family was no longer an economic necessity, it became instead a theological one.

These two roles of religion interacted with and supported each other. Nineteenth-century women were members of organized churches and there learned about the spiritual dimensions of their positions as wives and mothers. Their spirituality then led them to take up positions of moral superiority in society at large. That is, women

believed that the values they upheld in the home qualified them to organize for benevolence outside the home. As several historians note, "Implicit in such activism
was the conviction that the female experience represented a cultural alternative to
the materialism and competitive individualism of industrial capitalism."[18] Thus, the
Cult of Domesticity was not something that was confined to the home, but rather
extended to and influenced many aspects of wider society.[19]

Before the separation of spheres, Christian women in America were granted an avenue to God only through submission to their husbands. Women were viewed as lust-
ful, without soul, and prone to sin, and a Christian woman was dependent on her
husband for her relationship to the local church as well as to the state; the father
and husband was solely responsible for the spiritual nurture and welfare of his children. The ideological shift that accompanied industrialization taught that men
needed to be hardened and invulnerable to succeed in the world, and that women
therefore needed to be spiritually superior, especially when it came to the important
tasks of child rearing and housekeeping.[20] In the separation of spheres, men were
thought to be more aggressive, coldhearted, and self-interested, all traits needed
to function in the public sphere. It was precisely because women did not possess
these characteristics that they were thought to be superior. Although virtues traditionally associated with women, such as submission and obedience, are still present in the ideology of domesticity, they functioned in the Cult of Domesticity to en-
dow women with higher moral and spiritual status. The subjugation of women, as
Jane Tompkins aptly describes it, served to "enact a philosophy, as much political
as religious, in which the pure and powerless die to save the powerful and corrupt,
and thereby show themselves more powerful than those they save."[21] Thus, the
gendered theological hierarchy was reversed; whereas before, women were dependent on men for salvation, after the separation of spheres, a man could achieve a
sound relationship with God only through his wife and the safe haven she provided
at home.

The Cult of Domesticity left a strong theological legacy for American Christians, a
legacy that claims that Christianity is better when it is practiced inside a family with
a full-time mother. While a good number of social and liberation movements have
challenged the logic of separate spheres over the last century and half, this logic
pervades many aspects of Christian life today and remains fully intact in many conservative factions of Christianity.[22] As a result of the lasting effects of the cult of domesticity, we do not experience God as genderless people, but rather as men and

women; our gender dictates what kinds of experiences we can have with God, what kind of role we have in the living faith of our family, indeed even what positions and duties we can take up in church. The ideology of domesticity reconfigured American Christianity by locating theological and spiritual fulfillment only within those social units where both genders are represented, that is, only within the confines of the "traditional" family.

I suggest that the effects of the Cult of Domesticity and women's activity in nineteenth-century popular religion on theology are every bit as profound as those of Kant, Schleiermacher, and other nineteenth-century theologians and philosophers, because they made one's way of relating to God dependent on one's gender. Moreover, for the Christian Right, this system became the ideal model for the Christian family.

At the same time, however, this theology verified the importance of women only by ascribing to men the characteristics and authority necessary to fully control public, economic life. While men depended on women for their family-based relationship with God, women depended on men for material sustenance. Although the Cult of Domesticity did grant women an important and even life-sustaining role in the spiritual life of the family, in doing so it virtually guaranteed that women would not participate in public life. Any women who was spiritually equipped to direct her family to God would not have the proper constitution for negotiating and working in the harsh, heartless world of business.

The Cult of Domesticity continues to shape the way American Christians relate to God today. A glance at contemporary moral controversies reveals that the gender configurations set forth in the nineteenth century exist and are still being fought over today. It is not the case that Christians today think that women are unworthy of God or less spiritually equipped than men, formulations which preceded the nineteenth century. It is not the case that we understand gender as incidental to relationship with God. Rather, the debates that surround women's role in public life, paid labor, reproduction, abortion, and child rearing, as well as debates on the family's role in American culture, reflect the gendered convictions generated by the Cult of Domesticity. Women ought to stay at home, raise the family, and create a haven in the heartless world of the late twentieth century, conservative Christians argue, precisely because they are pure, pious, and relate to God more naturally. The public controversies that surround the role of women on the Christian Right are at their heart theological, because what is primarily at stake is how gender matters in a person's relationship with God.[23] By following the traces of the Cult of Domesticity over the course of the last century, it becomes even clearer that the contemporary conservative attitudes toward women and the family are extensions of nineteenth-century theological convictions.

The nineteenth-century Cult of True Womanhood had its drawbacks, as cultural analysts then and now are quick to point out. For example, Mary Ryan notes that while many women were engaged in progressive political struggles, membership in a church or voluntary organization alone did not guarantee such political activity. Ryan argues that many of the moral reform campaigns in which women participated ultimately served only to reinforce a program of limited social roles for women.[24] Ann Douglas argues that many nineteenth-century women were so caught up with sentimental drivel about home and family that they rarely showed awareness of the political consequences of reform activities.[25] Similar criticisms are leveled today against women of the contemporary Christian Right such as Phyllis Schlaffley, Marabel Morgan, Anita Bryant, and Beverly LaHaye.

Many nineteenth-century feminists also saw the limitations of the valorization of domesticity and concluded that the benefits won by the Cult of Domesticity were not worth the costs. While women's domestic and moral natures were valorized in the popular rhetoric, women, they believed, had little power in the public sphere. Early suffragists held the ideology of true womanhood up against the discourse of individualism and found the Cult of Domesticity wanting. They argued that America was founded on the ideals of liberty and justice for all individuals and saw the exclusion of blacks and women from these rights of citizenship as a violation of the promises entailed in the American dream. Many suffrage activists began their political involvement in the abolitionist movement.[26] On one level, their involvement in abolition was an extension of their participation in churches, voluntary organizations, and the moral reform movements just discussed. On another level, antislavery campaigns taught women that all citizens had legal and political rights as individuals. The ideology underpinning abolition contradicted the Cult of True Womanhood; that is, it was impossible to make the argument that women were equal while simultaneously arguing that they were inherently different. In the face of such contradiction many women abandoned the ideology of true womanhood in favor of an ideological project that extended individual freedom and rights to women, just as they had been extended to blacks.

At the same time, many nineteenth-century feminists began to associate the Cult of Domesticity with abuse and oppression of women in the home. Although the private sphere of home and family was viewed in the nineteenth century as a refuge from the cold world of business and industry, the home itself rarely received the benefits of justice regularly accorded to the public sphere. In many cases, the valorization of womanhood coexisted with serious persecutions of many wives and mothers. Women were associated with morality and spirituality only as long as they upheld the virtues of submission and obedience; if they refused to be submissive or obedient, they were often abused, abandoned, or institutionalized. Thus, in many cases, the haven associated with the home was intended only for men; for women, the home was simply a place to labor and to be oppressed.[27]

Suffragists were not the only women at century's end to register discontent with the Cult of Domesticity. By the beginning of the twentieth century, the "New Woman," although not actively involved in the campaign for the vote, tended to make choices that liberated her from the confines of domesticity. She often married later, often attended college, and as Carroll Smith-Rosenberg states, "repudiated the Cult of True Womanhood in ways her mother never could."[28] In the first decade of the twentieth century, Smith-Rosenberg argues, women began to be seen as full and equal citizens. Moreover, as Kathy Peiss forcefully demonstrates, these new ideologies about women's equality were not unique to middle and upper classes, but infiltrated working-class and immigrant women as well. Among them, the shift was displayed primarily through new kinds of social bondings; where friendships *between* women were most common in the Cult of Domesticity, the New Woman in all classes was demarcated, according to Peiss, by a turn to sexual and emotional bonds with men.[29] While assumptions about "women's superior nature" often lingered, the doctrine of women's difference was systematically challenged. Most importantly, under the influence of the New Woman, it came to be believed that women did not have to bear children, or for that matter even marry, to fulfill their womanly nature. Thus, many women began to follow their dreams into what was—a decade before—largely a male world.

By the 1920s, the dominant roles and attributes of American women had changed dramatically. Suffrage and the ideology of New Womanhood had achieved mainstream popularity and had opened new pathways for many women. Women began to go to college, to get professional training, and to take jobs at all levels of American industry. A sexual liberation simultaneously swept the country and more women had sex before marriage; indeed, some "flappers" even advocated sex with-out marriage. Divorce rates rose dramatically; the gendered theological heart of the Cult of Domesticity was being called into question. Women were leaving their homes and the domestic sphere in droves, and with that flight were abandoning what had become their theological responsibility: to provide a haven of morality and spirituality for their entire family.

These changes in gender caused simultaneous shifts in the economic sphere. As the ideology of New Womanhood drew women out of the home and into the workforce, families with two incomes were increasingly able to acquire material objects—from washing machines to automobiles—which signified their familial success. At the same time, the stay-at-home wife and mother was no longer a sign of economic suc-cess, because families with a wife and mother who worked at home without pay had a harder time keeping up with these signs of progress precisely because they didn't have that second income. In another economic shift, more women in the workforce meant a larger labor pool, more competition for existing jobs, and less job security for many men. Women often needed to work to support their families, and even at times their out-of-work husbands. These changes in the economic sphere had re-percussions not only on family life, but on the theology associated with the Cult of Domesticity as well.

In *Ungodly Women*, Betty DeBerg argues that the first wave of American fundamen-talism was one of the major opponents of these social and economic changes. In her extensive research on popular fundamentalist texts, she finds a common theme that demands the return of the Cult of Domesticity. For example, pleas found on posters such as the following bemoan the affairs of the New Woman and solicit women back into traditional, Victorian roles: "Wanted: more mothers, we are short on homes; real homes. We are short on mothers; real mothers. . . . God designed woman as the homemaker but somehow she seems to have gotten sidetracked."[30] DeBerg argues that the first fundamentalists increased their power and public ac-ceptance by demanding a return to nineteenth-century Victorian standards of gen-dered behavior. In so doing, fundamentalists posited a common enemy—the liber-ated woman—and turned to Christianity for the ammunition that would help put women back in the domestic sphere.

It wasn't only the suffragists' ideas about the nature of women that the fundamen-talists opposed;[31] it was also the way that everyday women across America were expressing these ideas in their actions. DeBerg finds page after page of exhortation such as the following passage from a 1926 Christian newsletter: "The Scriptures emphasize the active virtues in man.... In woman, they emphasize the passive virtues.... When this difference is lost and man becomes womanish, or woman becomes mannish, then the proper balance is lost, and harmony gives way to discord."[32] These assertions about Scripture and theology reorganized and reoriented the entire Christian message to support the return of the Cult of Domesticity.[33]

I suggest that the early fundamentalists embarked on this massive crusade because they saw having a stay-at-home wife and mother as the surest way to guarantee their vitally important relationship with God. Their reactions against women's liberation were a reaction against the changes in theological understanding that accompanied turn-of-the-century social and economic gender shifts. Specifically, if women held public jobs, performed in dance halls, and sometimes danced in scanty clothes that resembled underwear, then women—by their inherent nature—could not be pure and pious. And if women were not pure and pious, then their access to God—and their families' as well—was in jeopardy.

Like early fundamentalism, the contemporary Christian Right also relies on Scripture and various aspects of the Christian tradition to legitimate the theology behind the Cult of Domesticity and to attack women's departures from it. Indeed, the politics associated with contemporary Christian Right are driven by the fact that contemporary feminism threatens the gendered theology conceived in the Cult of Domesticity and nurtured in many fundamentalist and evangelical communities today. Conservative factions of American Christianity understand spirituality primarily as an attribute of women. Thus, when women become less interested in or willing to fill their natural, spiritual roles, contemporary conservative Christians respond like their ancestors with political agendas designed to return women to their natural sphere of domesticity. The aim of this backlash strategy is not to oppress women but to allow women to fulfill their God-given functions and to ensure the whole family's relationship to God.

The Christian Right's efforts to return women to the private sphere and to nineteenth-century gendered theology take a variety of forms. Conservatives oppose birth control and abortion so that Christian women who are able will bear large numbers of children. They oppose day care services to ensure that raising those children will be a full-time job. They promote home schooling, which virtually ensures that women will remain in the home re-creating the theological environment of the nineteenth century. Formulations that challenge this natural balance are deemed by the Christian Right to be unethical, unnatural, and ungodly.

Between the beginnings of Christian fundamentalism in the 1920s and the contemporary Christian Right, both fundamentalism and American life changed dramatically. In the first two decades of the twentieth century, fundamentalism reversed the political sentiments of its nineteenth-century evangelical ancestors. Whereas many nineteenth-century evangelicals were invested in progressive social reform movements such as temperance and abolition, early twentieth-century fundamentalists disassociated themselves from social progress movements.[34] By the end of the 1920s, yet another change took place: fundamentalism had ceased to contend for control of mainline denominations and had simultaneously withdrawn from many kinds of political involvement altogether. The Scopes trial of 1927, in which a law barring the teaching of evolution in the public schools was struck down, was a major defeat for fundamentalists; once it became apparent that fundamentalism's popularity was on the decline, as George Marsden put it, "the logic of their no compromise position pointed toward separatism."[35] The new separatist fundamentalism focused narrowly on the issues of Darwinism and Scriptural inerrancy and virtually ignored the expanding role women were experiencing in wider society.

Meanwhile, the role of women in public life and in the workforce underwent dramatic change, especially as a result of World War II. From 1942 to 1945, 4.7 million previously unemployed, predominately white, middle-class women entered the workforce, filling the positions that their husbands and brothers left when they went to war.[36] The American government responded to the changing needs of the American family in 1942 by spending $4 million in federal funds on public day care for the young children of working mothers. If fundamentalists noticed these changes, they did not seem to raise concerns about them, probably in order to support the war effort.

In 1945, however, the men came home; the white, middle-class women were sent home; the day care centers were closed; and American family life seemed to return to the domesticated balance that reigned a century earlier. The returned veterans—especially white, middle-class ones—were rewarded for their efforts with jobs, and fell into place as the breadwinners for the American family. Wives and girlfriends, happy to have their husbands home again, went back to the tasks of keeping the house and raising the children. Indeed, the social and economic life of America was restructured to support these domestic shifts. More and more families moved away from town and city centers and away from public transportation into the suburbs. While new roads and affordable cars were available to bring fathers to work, such moves often prevented women from keeping or seeking outside employment, because they could not earn a salary large enough to cover a second car, child care, and housekeeping expenses. In the isolated atmosphere of the suburbs, wives and mothers found and created more and more tasks designed to make their homes more pleasant places. America of the 1950s looked a lot like a Norman Rockwell painting and, changes in style and technology notwithstanding, the picture strongly resembled the families of their great-grandparents, with one exception: an unmistakable feeling of discontent.

The war had decisively altered delicate racial and gender balances. White and black men had fought side by side in battle, and women had taken up the slack in factories at home. The postwar culture of America tried to overcome and reverse these trends by policing the role of women and African-Americans. But as historian Wini Breines writes, "The postwar culture [of the 1950s] was a culture of containment, with women and black people its objects. . . . Anxiety over the loss of separate spheres and the integration of the sexes and races was articulated in the celebration of whiteness and traditional domestic femininity. The segregation of women from men and blacks from whites, their containment, took place under cover of an ideological consensus that was constructed as a way of staving off the claims of those who had been excluded."[37] Stated differently, the ideology of the 1950s strove to keep women and blacks out of the white, male workforce not through legislation, but through an ideology that valorized "traditional" family configurations. Songs, movies, magazines, television shows, and especially product commercials represented women as happiest when they were in the home, creating a domestic, suburban haven for their husbands and children. Men—who were now represented uniformly as sparkling white-collar workers—came home to their ranch homes in the suburbs and were pampered by a cleaner and better-decorated house, a gourmet meal, and a wife who had shifted her talents and energies out of the public workforce to the private realm of home. This pattern replicated completely the strategy of nineteenth-century separate spheres.

In the rhetoric of today's Christian Right, the 1950s are the golden age of Christian living. As Family Research Council (a conservative think tank) president Gary Bauer articulates it,

> *The decade that most pulls at our heartstrings is the 1950's . . . [a time when] Americans had a clear sense of what was right and what was wrong. These reliable standards permeated the whole society and were taught to children at home, church, and in the schools. From our earliest days books like McGuffy's readers and simple, homespun tales, such as the story of George Washington and the cherry tree, were passed on to children to instill simple values like honesty, truthfulness and integrity. Today we teach about ethics instead of teaching ethics themselves, we teach children decision making without suggesting what the decisions are that we hope and want them to make.*
>
> *The '50's was the decade before radical feminism. It was the decade of the baby boom and the growth of suburbia. The most controversial thing happening in popular culture was the argument about Elvis' swiveling hips. (It certainly seems like a quaint issue now.) Latchkey children, by and large, didn't exist. The school day routinely began with prayer. The illegitimacy rate was a tiny fraction of today's scandalous 27 percent rate. Abortion was permitted only in cases of rape and incest. No-fault divorce was still just a gleam in some reformer's eye. "Gay" meant happy, homosexuality was "in the closet," and placid "Ike" was in the White House. It was the decade of "Ozzie and Harriet" and "Father Knows Best."*[38]

It is interesting to note that when conservative Christians look back over American history, it is not the 1920s—when fundamentalism was in its heyday—that is valorized as the golden age. Rather it is the 1950s, a time when fundamentalism was absent from the public eye. I suggest that the 1950s operate as the pinnacle of American civilization for contemporary conservative Christians precisely because fundamentalism was unnecessary. That is, Americans in the 1950s had fully and effectively embodied the values of the Cult of Domesticity; it wasn't necessary for fundamentalists or conservative Christians to preach and teach that women ought to stay at home because women of the growing middle class were already doing so. The men and women of the 1950s knew their social places and more or less abided by these "naturally dictated" roles without the impetus of Scripture or the threat of eternal damnation. In short, the structure of social and economic life in the 1950s most closely resembled the way that God intended for men and women to live.

What this framework overlooks, however, is that the ideology of the 1950s was strong precisely because it was attempting to compensate for the instability brought on by war-related shifts in economics and gendered social patterns. The men and women of the 1950s were bombarded with Ozzie and Harriet images in the hopes that such representations would help to reorganize social life into more stable structures. When conservatives today look back on the 1950s, they fail to see the social disarray that representations of domestic harmony were intended to control. A decade before, women had worked outside the home, relied on public child care, and supported their children without their husbands. And even with Ozzie and Harriet on their new televisions, as it turned out, they were not happy with suburban isolation for long. The representations of the perfect, happy family that women and their families saw on television weren't quite enough to convince them that they were indeed happy.

Sexuality and its control is an important aspect of contemporary conservative ideology. By the 1940s, nonmarital and extramarital sex had become more common in many factions of the American public. But this standard changed at the end of the war when the watchwords of female sexuality—at least among most white, middle-class women—were *control* and *reputation*; a woman would forfeit her chance at the American dream if she lost either. According to Breines, "The culture was preoccupied with legitimate, meaning marital, sex, while other forms of sexuality were a source of shame, met by ignorance, fear, and punishment."[39] For women who had previously experienced a broader range of sexual and economic options, the constraints of the 1950s would ultimately prove too restrictive.

The first strong critique of "happy days" ideology came in 1963 with the publication of Betty Friedan's *The Feminine Mystique*. Friedan begins the book thus: "Gradually ... I came to realize that something is very wrong with the way American women are trying to live their lives today." Friedan called this "the problem that has no name," and claimed that "each suburban wife struggled with it alone."[40] She noticed that many (white, middle-class) women were marrying younger and more frequently and having more children, and that fewer women were finishing college or pursuing careers.[41] Girls, she noticed, were being sexualized and incorporated into the marriage market at earlier ages, while women actively marketed themselves for marriage. Friedan suggested that this behavior was driven by a mystique, that is, a belief that women were really happy. In her words,

The suburban housewife—she was the dream image of the young American women and the envy, it was said, of women all over the world. The American housewife—freed by science and the labor-saving appliances from the drudgery, the dangers of childbirth and the illnesses of her grandmother. She was healthy, beautiful, educated, concerned only about her husband, her children, her home. She had found true feminine fulfillment. As a housewife and mother, she was respected as a full and equal partner to man in his world. She was free to choose automobiles, clothes, appliances, supermarkets; she had everything that women ever dreamed of.

In the fifteen years after World War II, this mystique of feminine fulfillment became the cherished and self-perpetuating core of contemporary American culture. Millions of women lived their lives in the image of those pretty pictures of the American suburban housewife, kissing their husbands good-bye in front of the picture window, depositing their stationwagonsful of children at school, and smiling as they ran the new electric waxer over the spotless kitchen floor. They baked their own bread, sewed their own and their children's clothes, kept their new washing machines and dryers running all day. They changed the sheets on the beds twice a week instead of once, took rug-hooking class in adult education, and pitied their poor frustrated mothers who had dreams of having a career. Their only dream was to be perfect wives and mothers; their highest ambition to have five children and a beautiful house, their only fight to get and keep their husbands. They had no thought of the unfeminine problems of the world outside the home; they wanted men to make the major decisions. They gloried in their role as women, and proudly wrote on the census blank: "Occupation: housewife."[42]

The Feminine Mystique chronicled the costs of such deceptions. In her surveys of white, middle-class women in the suburbs, Friedan found that most American women were deeply dissatisfied with their limited roles as wives and mothers; she uncovered the pain involved when women came to the belief that "very little [of what they've done] has been really necessary or important." The solution to these problems, for Friedan, was for women to be aware of their own value. As she claimed, "Once [a woman] begins to see through the delusions of the feminine mystique—and realizes that neither her husband, nor her children, nor the things in the house, nor sex, nor being like all the other women, can give her a self—she often finds the solution much easier than she anticipated."[43] This would be brought about, Friedan thought, largely through education.

Friedan, of course, was not the only feminist to articulate dissatisfaction with the role of women in the 1950s.[44] Indeed, for many women and men today, the analysis contained in *The Feminine Mystique* seems almost quaint and certainly far from radical. However, the problems it described were real, and its articulation of them was revolutionary. I was seven years old when the book was published, and I was one of the countless baby boomer children that the 1950s system was intended to protect. My father went to work early every morning and my mother stayed at home with her children. I spent my days in the house and yard with my baby brother, helping my mother make cookies, sew our clothes, work on her home crafts, and cook dinner. I don't know if my mother ever read *The Feminine Mystique*, but I do remember that many times when I woke up early from my nap I found her crying. Friedan narrated the awakening to women's oppression in that era, as follows:

> On an April morning in 1959, I heard a mother of four, having coffee with four other mothers in a suburban development fifteen miles from New York, say in a quiet desperation, "the problem." And the others knew, without words, that she was not talking about a problem with her husband, or her children, or her home. Suddenly they realized they all shared the same problem, the problem that has no name. They began, hesitantly, to talk about it. Later, after they had picked up their children at nursery school and taken them home to nap, two of the women cried, in sheer relief, just to know they were not alone.[45]

My own mother eventually went to work when I went into the eighth grade, and although she had little education and probably hated the tasks associated with her secretarial job, she seemed much happier. It was her salary, she told me proudly, that eventually put me through college, and in many ways my accomplishments are extensions of her generosity and liberation.

I have a friend, just a few years younger than my mother, who did read *The Feminine Mystique*, and who was beaten by her husband when he found her reading it. Her husband beat her because he rightly understood that the ideology contained in that book—and the life changes that that ideology was prompting all over the nation— challenged the way he and his family lived. Many Christians who saw in the 1950s the kind of familial stability that was present in the Cult of Domesticity of their evangelical ancestors were threatened as well, not only by Friedan's or any other particular text that angered conservative Christians, but even more by the changes in gender that the text described.[46] By the late 1960s and early 1970s, many different kinds of feminists were challenging the logic that men were the uncontested heads of households, and the theology that was based on such gender ascriptions.

The texts of the Christian Right register discontent with these changes. The 1973 national bestseller *The Total Woman*, for example, addressed women who did not participate in these cultural changes, that is, those who chose to stay at home. Author Marabel Morgan offered strategies that would help women find happiness in a role that was beginning to lose viability for many Americans. Morgan began by describing a scene in which her husband often misused his power as head of household. Rather than exist in constant conflict with his authority, Morgan learned—she said—to get what she wanted out of life by using her femininity to her benefit. Morgan explored the moral importance of wives and mothers. She explained that women alone held the power to make family life happy, whether by making a good dinner or making herself sexually available to her husband:

> You have the power to lift your family spirit or bring it down to rock bottom. The atmosphere in your home is set by you. If you're cheery tonight, chances are your husband and children will also be cheery. If you're a crab, they probably will be too, since they take their cues for daily living from you.
>
> How is your attitude toward your daily duties? Are you pleasant to live with, even when your husband doesn't appreciate your efforts? Do you know your personal happiness depends on the attitude you decide you will have?[47]

Morgan's book (and the "Total Woman courses" that recreated the strategy of the book) taught housewives to manage their own unhappiness as part of their Christian duty. Morgan rightly understood that the traditional patriarchal family could only function when the woman is submissive not only to God but to her husband as well. "Starting tonight," Morgan prescribes, "determine that you admire your husband. By an act of your will, determine to fill up his cup, which may be bone dry."[48] With these and other pieces of advice, Morgan configured female submission in contemporary terms.

Morgan wrote for an audience of Christian women who were resisting feminist ideology by staying at home, and her book was meant to help these women live lives that were closer to the domestic ideal. The writings of conservative Christians in the 1990s make no such assumption; their target audience is not women who have chosen to stay at home, but women currently in the workforce who are thinking about leaving to become full-time wives and mothers. These new writers seek to persuade these readers that women are or are in danger of becoming more interested in their careers than in their families; that children are suffering because their mothers are at work rather than taking care of them; that divorce rates are up because women aren't fulfilling their roles as wives; and that the character of the nation is eroding because its families are no longer "intact." According to many on the Christian Right, the American family should make whatever sacrifices are necessary in order to keep the wife and mother at home, full-time.

"Most families do not need two paychecks," Operation Rescue founder Randall Terry claims. "In most of Middle America, people can make it on one income."[49] Head of the Family Research Council Gary Bauer claims that "the average woman contributes about 30 percent of the family income, not coincidentally, an amount just about equal to the federal and state tax burden on the typical family."[50] When child care costs are taken into account, the family comes out ahead, these works claim, when the wife stays at home. These books by men have been supplemented by an increasing number of books written by women who have rediscovered the joys of staying home. Brenda Hunter has appeared on *Larry King Live* and *Sally Jessy Raphael* to offer support and encouragement for mothers who choose to stay at home. "Our culture tells mothers they are not that important in their children's lives," she tells us, but this belief is wrong. "The Mother is the architect of intimacy. When we weaken attachments between mothers and children, all kinds of anomalies occur."[51] In Hunter's view, which is shared by many Christians in America, women should be in the home with their children. Such positions supply psychological and ideological support, as well as an economic rationale, for a return to the Cult of Domesticity. Mothers and wives stay at home and reproduce daily life for husbands and children as a function of their inherent nature and as part of their Christian duty.[52]

Susan Faludi has persuasively argued that men on the Christian Right oppose women working outside the home not only because women are then not available to serve men and children, but also because when women are out in the workforce, they are competing for—and winning—many of the positions previously occupied by men. As women experience improvements in their social and economic positions, the Christian Right responds with, as Faludi describes it, backlash ideology.

> Men (on the Christian right) are hurting from severe economic social dislocations in their lives—changes that they so often blamed on the rise of independent and professional women. As they lost financial strength at work and private authority at home, they saw women gaining around the office, challenging control of the family at home, and even taking the initiative in the bedroom. . . . [Many of the men associated with the Christian Right] belong to the second half of the baby boom generation, [they] not only missed the political entrenchment of the sixties but were cheated out of the era's affluent bounty. They are downwardly mobile sons, condemned by the eighties economy to earning less than their fathers, unable to buy homes or support families. . . . These are the men who are losing ground and at the same time see women gaining it—and suspect a connection.[53]

From this perspective, the rhetoric that attempts to keep women at home and out of the workforce has a socioeconomic aim.

However, it is not only men who react negatively to women working outside the home; conservative women participate in the backlash as well. They do so because they are equally anxious about their tenuous positions in the gendered theological system. If society accepts the feminist assertion that women are not spiritually and morally superior to, but rather equal to men, many conservative women would lose their material security; if women are not allowed to provide a "haven in a heartless world," they will be thrust into the heartless world themselves and will perish.[54] As Mrs. Ruth Bell Graham, wife of Billy Graham, describes the feeling, "The women's liberation movement is turning into men's liberation because we are freeing them from their responsibilities. I think we are being taken for a ride."[55] For these women, the move toward equality between the sexes destabilizes what they perceive to be the powerful position women hold in society. From their viewpoints, women who stay at home are freed from the labor force in order to do the really important work of God. Changes that threaten this order also threaten "the abundant life God has planned especially for women."[56]

For many conservative women, the greatest security women can have is found within the system whereby relationship with God depends on gender, and where every family needs a woman to secure theological connection. The feminist struggle to provide women with equal access to employment actually degrades women, as well as functioning, as Beverly LaHaye puts it, "[to] confuse [women's] priorities, to shortchange their homes and families, and [to] totally exhaust the women themselves."[57] The best plan for women is to stay home, for it is there, conservatives believe, that women can exert the greatest Christian influence. As Pat Robertson says, "We've got to come back to the point of Christian marriage, Christian childcare, Christian families, and we've got to come to the point where being a housewife is a noble profession and not something that's sneered at and looked down on by emancipated ladies. That's very important. Who rules our nation? Who is going to determine the next generation? It's not going to be the politicians and the presidents and the senators and judges—it's going to be the mothers."[58]

Moreover, contemporary conservative theorists are trying to make the home a more attractive place by avoiding the pitfalls that plagued the 1950s. They recognize that one of the major problems stay-at-home wives and mothers face today is isolation. The isolation of women in the suburbs in the 1950s created fertile ground for feminist ideas; today's conservative women attempt to correct this problem by advocating connections between women. "You and I need to make a great effort to develop friendships," Beverly LaHaye writes, "because we are swimming against a powerful tide. Generations ago women spent a great deal of their lives with other women as they engaged in daily tasks related to the home, but today there is no need for us to congregate routinely." By advocating female friendship and connection, contemporary conservative women implicitly acknowledge that the image of the 1950s "happy days" culture was superimposed on a world of isolation and discontent for women. When women do not feel isolated or angry, the whole system functions better. Or as LaHaye writes, "If a woman does not receive affirmation from other women, it will be all the more difficult for her to be secure in her relationships with men."[59]

For conservative Christians, gender dictates one's place in the economic, social, and spiritual system of the Christian Right. Despite the restrictive view of women's role embraced by the Right, many women feel secure within the fold of conservative Christianity. As Margaret Bendroth explains, "Women, like men, found a clear, though perhaps narrow, call to Christian vocation and a language of cultural critique that simplified the daunting range of choices in a secular lifestyle. Women perhaps especially appreciate the movement's high standards for family life. . . . [The Christian Right] upholds women's role in the family and even more important, provide[s] a forum for like-minded women to air common fears and hopes for their children."[60]

Indeed, for any woman who has ever tried to find a job in an economy with high unemployment or struggled with the often competing demands of a career and family, the idea of staying at home and daily re-creating a "haven in a heartless world" is sometimes attractive. The strategies and the rhetoric of the Right should not be dismissed as innocuous or retrograde precisely because there are times in our lives when they make sense. The Right narrates a story about women's spiritual power that is extremely seductive, and it is for this reason that the logics and consequences of the Right must be examined and evaluated.

The desire to know God always emerges within an interpretive paradigm. That is, we do not seek God independent of community and experience, but rather as a result of some encounter. For some Christians on the Left, for example, God is discovered in relationship to liberation. For many Christians on the Right, God is known primarily through gender. That is, just as in nineteenth-century ideology, conservative Christian women need men for material sustenance; conservative Christian men need women to re-create the spirituality associated with home. Male-female relationships are crucial because, as Gary Bauer says, "men and women need each other to share their lives together and to build a better future."[61] Neither men nor women alone have complete access to God. Men need women to have a successful relationship with God, and women need men to support the family so that they may stay at home and develop their spiritual and moral sensibilities. The single life, therefore, is rarely seen as a viable and permanent choice.[62]

This gendered system of theology both reflects and prescribes attitudes about the gender of God. Before the middle of the nineteenth century, it made some sense for all people to be called "man" or "mankind" and for God to be called "father" because the father of the preindustrial family was a representative of his whole household. When someone referred to the father of the house, it was understood that this figure represented more human beings than just himself. Only adult men with property were granted the right to vote, for example, as they were thought to represent their wives, children, and slaves. It was appropriate, then, that husbands would represent their wives because women were thought to be less than men. Women could not vote or own property, as it was believed that they were ontologically closer to animals than to men and that they did not have souls.[63]

Theologically, the Cult of Domesticity bridged the gap between a time when women were thought of as less than human and a time when women were thought of as both fully human and equal to men. In the ideology of domesticity, women were seen as different but not inferior; indeed, as I have demonstrated, women were seen as morally and spiritually superior to men. God remained "father" in the Cult of Domesticity not because women were inferior or like animals, but rather because women were primarily the people who had relationships with God. Within a system that requires that opposite genders complement each other, if the most spiritual kind of human beings are women, then God, by logic, must be male. Conservatives today extend into the present these nineteenth-century theological convictions about the importance of the fatherhood of God.

Today, most Americans no longer believe that the father represents, rules, or stands in for other members of his family; indeed, good fathers today eschew such authoritarian roles. Similarly, most women do not think of ourselves as morally or spiritually superior to men. However, although many Christian denominations have introduced gender-neutral and feminine language for God into their liturgies, the exclusive use of masculine names and images for the divine is virtually uncontested on the right.[64]

The fatherhood of God is so important to conservatives because much would be lost, theologically and spiritually, if women were treated as fully equal to men. If conservatives liberated women from their current gender roles, they would lose their relationship with the god they call "father." Although those of us who exist outside this gendered theology see other ways of relating to and understanding God, conservatives themselves do not. To them, God is "father," and the naturalness and necessity of earthly gendered roles verifies this fact. Moreover, the reverse is also true. If the Christian Right were to change God's name from "father" to "creator" or "parent," if God were understood as being not male, then women would no longer have special spiritual roles, and there would be no reason (based solely on their gender) for them to stay at home. Men and fathers could just as easily do the work of child care, housekeeping, and building family life. Thus, the system of gendered theology fixes not only the social roles of Christian men and women, but the gender of God as well.

Because gender is the first organizing category for conservative theology, females are initially sorted from males; femaleness and the home exist on one side, maleness and public work exist on the other. The two categories meet only on the terms of the heterosexual family, the entity that grounds the whole system. In this system where God is male, women relate to God directly, and men can only know God one step removed. In using the heterosexual family as the model for Christian theology, the ideology of domesticity constructs and verifies the idea that heterosexuality and the nuclear family are both necessary and intrinsic to human existence. If God is the father and women are responsible for conducting that relationship, then the family, the home, and the heterosexual relationship appear to mimic the most holy way of negotiating life.

In this paradigm, the maleness of Christ becomes central to his existence. And because God, Jesus Christ, and all men are on one side of the paradigm, they influence and affect each other in a way that women—who are on the opposite side—cannot and do not. In the thinking of the Right, while women are primarily in charge of their family's relationship with God, men—and especially fathers—represent God the father and the historically male Christ.[65] Thus, conservative Jay Adams writes, "When a husband fails he mars the image of our Lord in a peculiar way in which the wife cannot."[66]

This system of gendered theology not only affects our perceptions of God's gender and nature; it also influences discussions about ordination and leadership roles within churches. In the pre-nineteenth-century cultural climate that understood the male as the representative of and for the family, only men were ordained because only men could represent God. Some factions of the Christian Right maintain this ideology. As Susan Foh articulates it: "God has forbidden the teaching and ruling offices in the church to women, and he has appointed the husband the head of the wife. . . . By creating the man first, God established him as the head of the human race. There is a sense in which the woman is included in the man, is represented by him, but the reverse is not true. And so in the one-flesh union, the husband is the head; the male elders in the church can represent the whole congregation—men and women."[67]

Most factions of the contemporary Christian Right, however, have extended the more confused gendered theology of the Cult of Domesticity into discussions of women's ordination today. When viewed from one perspective, the ideology of the Cult of Domesticity taught that women were spiritually superior, and therefore welcomed their interpretation of the Christian message. During and as a result of the Cult of Domesticity in America, women such as Phoebe Palmer (a revival preacher who had a long-lasting effect on Methodism), Catherine Booth (founder of the Salvation Army), and Hannah Whitehead Smith (founder of the Keswick Conference) took up formal and informal positions of leadership in the church and preached the

Christian message in a sustained and powerful manner. As one writer notes, "The high priority placed on [women's] spiritual gifts left the door ajar for women in ministry."[68] However, although Palmer, Booth, Smith, and others left significant marks on American religious history, most preaching women were part of husband-wife teams, in which only the husband was officially ordained or recognized by the denomination. In fact, women who lived in the Cult of Domesticity could *not* be independently ordained (unless they were members of certain small religious groups such as Quakers, Unitarians, or Universalists), and therefore were treated unequally and unfairly. If women wanted to be involved in the life of the church, they were forced to do so outside the traditional structures of authority, and often relied on their husbands for formal links to denominations. In this sense, the older logic which denied women ordination ruled.

As a result of conservative Christianity's entrenchment in the ideology of the Cult of Domesticity, most conservative evangelical traditions refused to grant women orders well into the twentieth century. As Bonnidell and Robert Clouse note, "In contrast to mainline denominations [which began to ordain women ministers early in the twentieth century], the evangelical movement which developed between 1920 and 1960 discouraged female leadership. Reacting to the social gospel, these conservatives turned back to a literal understanding of the Bible."[69] Such passages as 1 Corinthians 14:34–35 ("Women should keep silence in the churches. For they are not permitted to speak, but should be subordinate.") are still used by conservative Christians to keep women from public leadership.

Recent scholarship in American religious history points out that evangelicals and fundamentalists have not been entirely consistent in their reactions to women in positions of power. Bendroth notes that in many factions of conservative fundamentalism, the ideology of the Cult of Domesticity eventually gave way to the patriarchal constructions that preceded it. As she puts it, "By the 1920s fundamentalism had adopted the belief that it was men, not women, who had true aptitude for religion."[70] Other scholars note that despite Scriptural references that excluded women from formal ministerial positions, women were very involved in early fundamentalism in nontraditional ways. Michael Hamilton, for example, demonstrates that women took up active roles in many factions of fundamentalism before 1950. "Fundamentalists did hold marriage in high regard, many of their books and magazines lauded the virtues of a godly home attended by a wife." But "this was nearly always subordinated to the larger concern that all young men and women experience personal conversion, live selfless lives wholly dedicated to God, and enter some kind of full-time Christian service."[71] Women's leadership was permitted, but only if it was guided by God's higher authority.

This is certainly the case of the women in positions of public leadership today. Although many women participate in the public ministry as an extension of their involvement with the spiritual and moral duties associated with child rearing and homemaking, most gain their access to public ministry through their husbands. On the national level, Tammy Faye Bakker, Macel Falwell, Ruth Bell Graham, Maude Aimee Humbard, Evelyn Roberts, Arvella Schuller, Beverly LaHaye, and Frances Swaggart all played very active roles in their husbands' ministries. Frances Swaggart outlined her involvement: "People would be most surprised to learn that I play as large a role in the ministry as I do. I work in every phase of the ministry and everybody answers to me. I know where all the money goes. I get reports every day, and I go through every one." Swaggart's participation is not extraordinary. Some wives fill in as hosts on their husbands' television shows, while others control various aspects of the ministry. In one sense, these women work in these ministries to fulfill their commitment to God; as Hamilton puts it, "to live selfless lives wholly dedicated to God," or as Rex Humbard's wife says, "The Lord spoke to me and said 'Soldier, I have a job for you to do.'"[72] On the other hand, however, these women only have access to the airwaves through their husbands and by virtue of the fact that the role of wife and mother in conservative Christian circles is valorized. Thus, in the logic of domesticity, a woman is allowed to speak, but only from within a complicated web of domestic and cultural dynamics.

These faithful and loving Christian wives exemplify the kind of controlled power that women have within the ideology of the Cult of Domesticity. That is, today's conservative woman ought first to be a wife and mother; she may participate in the public sphere only if it advances the Christian message and only with her husband's permission. In such a paradigm, a woman working for money or for her own power is unthinkable. Conservative Christianity responded to contemporary feminism not only by producing manuals that attempted to keep women happy in the home, but also with a myriad of public models that demonstrated that the most satisfying and spiritual place for women was at their husbands' sides.

The Right's outrage at Hillary Clinton's participation in national government both illustrates and reinforces this boundary. Most conservative commentators believe that Hillary has far outstepped the role of wife; Texe Marrs, author of *Big Sister Is Watching You*, claims that "Hillary Rodham Clinton is not just co-President of the United States—she's the real power in Washington, D. C. And to help her run the big show, Hillary has brought in lesbians, sex perverts, child molester advocates, Christian haters, and the most doctrinaire of communists." According to Marrs—who is one among many Christian detractors—Hillary and these women are involved in a plot to take over the government and overthrow family values in favor of "the radical feminist agenda." As Marrs states his most pressing concern, "The women of the New World Order will change the way we think about God."[73]

Precisely. Women like Hillary Clinton who work outside the home and compete in public spaces alongside men are changing the way many Christians think about God. When restrictive notions of gender are challenged, God can be understood not as a gendered person "himself," but rather as a loving creator and sustainer who transcends the socially organized gender systems developed on earth. When earthly gender codings no longer restrict us, we are free to negotiate different relationships with a loving, nongendered God.

For both male and female members of the Christian Right, these changes are threatening because the God who transcends or steps out of conventional gender patterns is utterly unrecognizable. The Right, then, has launched a full-scale initiative to denigrate women like Hillary Clinton who work outside the home and hold positions of power in society, and to return to the nineteenth-century order whereby theological relationships are dictated by gender. The social consequences of this for women are enormous; in this theological strategy, women wield less social power, make less money, and leave fewer marks on history than men do. Although this gendered theological anthropology might allow women to have deeper and more significant relationships with God, these relationships come at material cost. The Right responds to women's material oppression and containment by deemphasizing social power, material resources, and historical impact. In focusing solely on spiritual power, the Right overlooks the current and very real socioeconomic discrimination against women. What women need and want, I suggest, is both access to God *and* social and economic justice; any model which sets these two up as competing or mutually exclusive claims is unsatisfactory.

What stands behind the contemporary revival of the Cult of Domesticity is a theologically valid concern: the desire to know God. However, when we genderize our relationship with God, we enmesh ourselves in a series of problems that lead ulti-mately to the socioeconomic oppression of women. The Right believes that the only way to have relationship with God is through gender; in doing so, it dismisses con-cerns about material oppression and reinterprets women's role as mother and housewife as natural, fulfilling, even liberating. Christian women today need a world where both staying at home and going out to work are viable, theological op-tions. The gendered theology associated with the Cult of Domesticity is liberating and valorizing only for those women who work at home with their house and chil-dren; many forms of feminism—both secular and Christian—valorize only those women who go out to work. We need a theology that can see the value of both op-tions, in which spiritual nourishment is not dependent on the way that gender is configured.

The Right's gendered theology oppresses men in other ways. Although they usually have control over the material future of their wives and families, men report that they often feel overburdened with expectations about what they can and should do as fathers, husbands, and Christian men.[74] Stated simply, they must provide the family income so that the wife can stay home full-time. Moreover, in concrete ways their spiritual relationships are dependent on women. In terms of church affiliation, this logic turns back on itself; that is, because spirituality is associated with women, men must work hard to masculinize their involvement in the Church.[75] Thus, men al-most entirely dominate more formal, visible, well-paid tasks such as producing the-ology, leading in large churches, and denominational administrating.

The gender attributes described in this chapter have prompted many Christians for the last 150 years to organize themselves into families. That is, although indus-trialization brought with it economic changes such that people could live inde-pendently, the majority of people chose to live their lives inside a family unit. Since industrialization, however, the shape of the American family has changed dramati-cally: where once *family* meant a group of people with varying degrees of blood rela-tions who shared living space and household chores, for the last hundred years *fam-ily* has come to mean *only* a heterosexual couple and their biological or adopted children. In the American family today, we see fewer unmarried aunts and uncles, fewer orphaned cousins, fewer elderly grandparents sharing space with a "real" family. In contemporary conservative ideology, all any family needs is a mother to stay home and attend to the moral and spiritual needs of the children, a father to bring home a paycheck, and a reasonable number of children. In this logic, this small family unit is complete; indeed, additional members are often explicitly unwelcome precisely because they could upset the delicate balance. The expense of an elderly grandparent, for example, might necessitate a second income. Moreover, the presence of an elderly relative might also mean free and reliable child care so that a mother would have little reason not to work outside the home if extra money was needed. In the logic of these nuclear families, two adults are not only enough, but all the system can bear.

Basing theology on gender also increases the importance of gender in all areas of life, leading finally to a system in which all social and theological roles are connected to one's genitals. In this interpretation of Christianity, anyone who does not fit the paradigm of their biological sex, (including working women and "sensitive" or disabled men as well as homosexuals), is excluded from the church.

The exercise of knowing God through gender has led the Right into a tangle of problems that has crystallized over the last decade into a full-blown war, a war that is sited on the family. The family has become the method for securing gendered theology. Moreover, the Christian Right has made the meaning and use of family the most important theological question we face. Many conservative Christians today seek God primarily in relation to family. The rhetoric of family is not an answer to a particular question raised by God or the Bible. Rather, the configuration of the traditional family is itself the vehicle that leads these Christians to God. Thus, the rhetoric of family values is particularly dangerous, because what most people think they're doing in using it is seeking and (they believe) finding God.

CHAPTER THREE

Sexuality, Salvation, and the Campaign for Family Values

The family is the fundamental building block and basic unit of our society and its continued health is a prerequisite for a healthy and prosperous nation.

James Dobson

Heterosexuality secures its self-identity and shores up its ontological boundaries by protecting itself from what it sees as the continual predatory encroachment of its contaminated other, homosexuality.

Diana Fuss

One of the most telling events of the 1992 presidential campaign illustrates the Christian Right's concerns about both gender roles and sexual behavior. Understanding the Christian Right's interest in sexual purity, as well as its belief in American exceptionalism and its theology of the end times, is necessary to comprehend the vigorous antigay rhetoric that dominates the Right's discourse and influences American conversations about homosexuality.

In his May 19, 1992, address to the San Francisco Commonwealth Club, then Vice President Dan Quayle stated that "it doesn't help matters when prime time T.V. has Murphy Brown—a character who supposedly epitomizes today's intelligent, highly paid, professional woman—mocking the importance of fathers, by bearing a child alone, and calling it just another 'lifestyle choice.'" Quayle attacked the creators of the sitcom because, as he later stated in *Standing Firm*, "I was bothered by all the cute glamour with which the episode (sure to be seen by millions of young girls and boys) was being surrounded.... My main objection was to how the show deemed fathers irrelevant—in a way that was damaging above all to children. Fathers are important to a child's life—both financially and emotionally." The overwhelming response to this comment prompted Quayle to continue to criticize "the cultural elite" who, as he put it, "sneer at the simple but hard virtues—modesty, fidelity, sexual purity."[1] His criticisms of the fictional Murphy Brown and single mothers in general illustrated the growing concern among conservatives for "family values," and revealed precisely how far the criticism of "alternate" lifestyles reached.

Quayle's remarks, and the multitude of media responses to them, capture two of the Right's main concerns about the social organization of family life. On the one hand, Quayle believed that, because Murphy Brown had a child without being married to its father, she challenged the gender ascriptions articulated in the last chapter. As conservative talk show host Rush Limbaugh said, "The real message of the Murphy Brown episode was that women don't need men, shouldn't desire them, and that total fulfillment and happiness can be achieved without men or husbands."[2] In a similar vein, conservative leader Gary Bauer noted that "Vice-President Quayle was right on the money.... Children are beginning life without fathers. Their mothers are beginning family life without husbands. The situation is tragic."[3] In the thinking of the Right, without the complementarity of a husband— that is, without a man's income—Murphy Brown is forced to continue working out-side the home and therefore jeopardizes her superior moral and spiritual status. Al-though Murphy Brown is wealthy, and can provide for her child, the baby will still be born into a disadvantaged position without the complementarity of a mother *and* a father.

Quayle also found fault with Murphy Brown because she, like many other women in America today, had obviously had sex outside of marriage. As Bauer states, "If we care about this society, we will do all we can to cease depicting out-of-wedlock sex as rewarding."[4] For the contemporary Right, sexual abstinence outside of mar-riage has become critically important; relationships with God depend not only on having the right balance of sexes in a marriage, but also on keeping sexual activity confined to that marriage. Manuals for Christian approaches to sexual abstinence outside of marriage fill the shelves of Christian bookstores and are regularly coun-ted among Christian bestsellers. The Murphy Brown incident indicates that sexual purity is thought to be a virtue for people of all ages.

Promoting abstinence among young people, however, receives particular empha-sis. Focus on the Family's James Dobson, for example, writes in *Dare to Discipline* that he and his wife took their daughter to an expensive restaurant, gave her a neck-lace with a gold key, and challenged her to remain a virgin until her wedding night. Other Christian parents have followed Dobson's lead and challenged their own chil-dren to remain chaste until marriage, to make a "commitment to virtue." Dobson repeatedly preaches the point that "no one has ever been hurt by refraining from sexual expression."[5] Conservative champion Tim LaHaye claims that his most im-portant success was raising two daughters in southern California who were virgins on their wedding day. LaHaye expresses just how dangerous sex outside of marriage is by exhorting, "Except for drug addiction nothing can ruin a teenager's life faster or more completely than premarital sexual activity (the two often go together)."[6] Major conservative Christian campaigns today attempt not only to remove sex education from public schools, but to train parents to educate their children at home about the value of abstinence over birth control.

It is not only adults who advocate sexual purity; many Christian teens across America organize themselves into abstinence support groups. A national network of pro-abstinence teens sponsors an annual "True Love Waits" rally which in 1994 claimed over 100,000 participants.[7] Indeed, from the perspective of many Christian teens, the movement to keep sexual encounters confined to marriage constitutes the heart of Christian sexual ethics. The campaign for sexual purity among unmarried Christians of all ages, then, is widely accepted by many factions of the conservative Christian population as the backbone of Christian moral teaching.

This emphasis on Christian purity, to be sure, is in part a response to the threat of AIDS and to the several sexual revolutions that have occurred over the last three decades, with accompanying changes in social mores and media representations of sexual activity. The Christian Right reacts against these changes by insisting that sex is moral only inside marriage. However, conservative Christianity's emphasis on purity is also intricately connected to theological concerns in general and specifically to the gendered theology presented in the last chapter. Although the relationship between sexuality and Christianity is a long and complicated one, it is the developments related to the Cult of Domesticity that serve as the theological foundation for the contemporary Christian campaign for purity.

Prior to the industrialization of America, a rural family unit needed many children to work on the farm and perform the tasks necessary to reproduce daily life. As America became industrialized, however, children became less of an asset and more of a burden. As people moved to towns and cities and were supported by wages rather than by products grown on farms, families could support fewer children. Especially if they hoped to maintain middle-class status, couples needed to limit reproduction. However, in an era when birth control was either nonexistent or unreliable, limiting reproduction was not an easy task.[8]

The ideology of the Cult of Domesticity that helped women cope with the economic changes by valorizing the work associated with the home also addressed the prob-

lem of fertility by granting women control over the sexual domain. That is, a new discourse about sexuality and romantic love emerged, in which women—as part of
their spiritually and morally superior nature—were encouraged to control the number and type of sexual encounters they had with their husbands. This emerging ideology reconfigured sex itself as a sinful act of lust; it cast sexual desires as one of
the more degrading of human needs. Only women could make sex right by surrounding it with romance and purity. Sex, under their control, was transformed into
a sweet, sensitive, dainty act, which the larger population could then accept. Outside of marriage, this transformation could not take place. Sex was only acceptable,
the Victorians claimed, when it occurred within the framework of romantic love and
marriage, and women were enlisted to police the boundary between love and lust.
Women, then, wielded a great amount of power in the ordering of sexual activity,
and were thus able to limit the number of sexual encounters within a marriage (and
consequently to regulate the number of children they conceived).

As part of this larger logic of regulation, women's control over sex meant that the
act became filled with spiritual significance. As Steven Seidman suggests, "[The
Victorians] were convinced that sexual expression automatically elicits lust, which
carries personal and social dangers. [They] responded by organizing an intimate
culture that attempted to control and spiritualize lust. Sexual expression was legiti-
mated only within a heterosexual, coitus-centered marital norm. As the campaigns
against masturbation and the moral effort to spiritualize sex and marriage indicate,
Victorian intimate culture sought to affirm sex expression while purging it of its carnal aspects."[9] Thus, where sex outside of marriage was thought to be fundamentally sinful, sex inside marriage was "the human manifestation of one's love of
God."[10] Women's sexual feelings were thought to be less related to sinful lust and
more related to the spiritual realm of nurturance and care. The concept of "romance" which arose during this period regulated sexual activity by placing women
in charge of this romantic love; the association between women, romance, and love
remade encounters into spiritual events and thus established romantically based
sexual activity as one aspect of the (spiritually superior) woman's domain. While romantic love did not replace sexual activity, it did help women control it by creating
an ideological space in which women could demand certain emotions and affecta-
tions. Women controlled sex, then, not only to limit the number of conceptions, but
also to verify and demonstrate their higher spiritual authority. Sex became the ter-
rain on which women confirmed that they were closer to God.

This emphasis on romance became firmly attached to the theological gender roles discussed in the last chapter, which have continued to influence the Christian Right. The many romance manuals produced by the conservative Christians emphasize the importance of romance to marriage in ways that fit the specific and assigned gender roles already in place. In keeping with the complicated position of women in the Cult of Domesticity, women "need" romance more than men do, but it is that very romance that keeps the family alive. James Dobson claims, for example, that "romance is linked to self-esteem in women. For a man, romantic experiences with his wife are warm and enjoyable and memorable—but not necessary. For a woman they are her lifeblood. Her confidence, her sexual response, and her zest for living are often directly related to those tender moments when she feels deeply loved and appreciated by her man."[11] Romantic love provides the firm foundation for a Christian family as well as a satisfying sex life. These manuals and the relationships they help produce not only reinforce women's spiritual and moral superiority; they also emphasize that good and moral sex is available only within the confines of committed, heterosexual marriage.

Although romance and sex are confined to heterosexual marriage in this paradigm, the discourse of romance demonstrates that conservative Christians are not opposed to sex per se. Christian romance manuals often contain detailed descriptions of sexual acts and may even function within those communities as a kind of erotica. In portraying sex within marriage so vividly, these books show that conservative Christians are not prudish or puritanical when it comes to sex, as long as it takes place inside marriage, a circumstance that supports the theological differences between genders.[12] The romance narrative that undergirds this endorsement of sex within marriage works to keep gender the primary category for relating to God.

These ideas—along with the "traditional family" they produce—are fueled not by Scripture, creed, or known Christian heritage but rather by an image created by 1950s television. As Stephanie Coontz argues, "Our most powerful visions of traditional families derive from images that are still delivered to our homes in countless reruns of 1950s television sitcoms." When the Right imagines and characterizes the traditional family, it is almost always in terms of *Ozzie and Harriet, Leave it to Beaver, The Andy Griffith Show, Father Knows Best, My Three Sons*, and later, *Little House on the Prairie*, and *The Waltons*. Although the specifics vary from series to series, these shows collectively signal an image of family in which fathers labor outside the home, mothers are in charge of spiritual and moral life inside the home, and children are obedient and never display sexual feelings until after they are married.[13] Although these programs depict families in several different historical periods, they are all a product of the 1950s ideology that organized postwar people back into nineteenth-century gendered theology. The goal of these shows was to impose stability and structure onto an era that was deeply dissatisfied with prescribed gender roles. While these images and narratives were unable to stave off the sexual changes associated with the 1960s and 1970s, they were instrumental twenty-five years later in organizing the core conception of the traditional family for the Right's family values campaign.

The Right understood that these television shows, when broadcast in conjunction with religious programming, could assist their campaign to organize conservative Christians into families that stood for sexual purity and stay-at-home motherhood. Thus, when Pat Robertson's Christian Broadcasting Network (CBN) began broadcasting full-time in the early 1980s, it filled its open time slots not with other television preachers (as previous full-time religious channels had done) but with movies and sitcoms from the 1950s. As Robertson discussed his decision not to program only religious shows, he said, "People might enjoy steak, but they don't want to eat it 24 hours a day. There has to be certain variety and activity and pace, and even the most devout I don't think want to watch hard religious programs hour after hour. . . . They need shows that will make them laugh."[14] Robertson's strategy of interspersing religious programming with *Ozzie and Harriet* and shows like it gave viewers a sense of what the traditional family, the moral model Robertson's religious shows hailed, looked like and how it functioned in daily life.

Robertson's CBN and other religious and "family" channels such as INSP and The Family Channel began televising the reruns and simultaneously telling viewers that the family life associated with the 1950s was the height of Christian living in America.[15] As one of Robertson's aides claimed, "We're not really here to get into politics. We're here to turn the clock back to 1954 in this country."[16] As part of the campaign to associate Christian morality with adherence to this televised image of the 1950s, James Dobson made the following comments in one of his mass-mailed newsletters:

> *The idea of saving oneself for marriage in 1954 made a lot of sense. Morality was fashionable. Students who slept around were disrespected by their peers. It*

never occurred to us that virginity was a curse to be gotten rid of, or that adults expected us to copulate like animals in heat. That crazy idea would come along in the modern era, when everyone from the school nurse to our misguided surgeon general seemed to be chanting, "Do it often. Do it right. Use a condom every night."

[Liberals] have mocked the families of the 1950s calling them repressive, authoritarian and rather silly, like "Ozzie and Harriet." They prefer the acerbic feminism of Murphy Brown, brazenly bearing a baby out of wedlock. Before we ridicule the way families and culture used to be, let me offer an eyewitness account from a teenager who was there in 1954. It was a very good year.[17]

Beginning in the late 1970s, the Right's campaign for family values quickly embraced much more than instructing Christians to imitate the family models of 1950s television. Its leaders argued that the sexual revolutions of the 1960s had contributed significantly to the "decline" of American culture, and that America would only be restored if it returned to the domestic arrangements of the 1950s. Through a logic explored later in this chapter, the family values campaign became linked with a desire to return America to its traditional Christian heritage, and this joint struggle compelled conservative Christians to participate in various sorts of public, political arenas. From their perspective, America had been founded as a Christian nation, but secular humanists and sexual liberationists had corrupted it. The decision to fight these cultural changes through party politics was a departure from the tradition of most conservative Christians over the last century, who had kept out of national politics in favor of a more separate, sectarian profile. By contrast, contemporary conservatives felt that the political realm was the most important place in which the values of home, motherhood, and the family could be protected. The campaign for family values was thus exported out of the homes of the new traditional families and brought into the arena of national politics.

In January 1979, Jerry Falwell, a southern fundamentalist preacher, met with conservative representatives who persuaded him that America would never fully realize its Christian potential until the morality of the nation was restored. By forming the Moral Majority later that year, Falwell hoped to persuade those Christian Americans who believed that abortion, homosexuality, premarital sex, gambling, and women's liberation were immoral to organize themselves. In so doing, Falwell was the first major evangelical to translate Christian action into conservative political involve-

ment. To be an evangelical Christian in America, according to Falwell's Moral Majority, meant joining forces with party politics to eradicate immoralities such as abortion. In the years that followed, this affiliation was to shape the character of both
the Republican Party and evangelical Christianity.

Evangelicals had already begun to get involved with party politics in the 1976 election of born-again Christian Jimmy Carter. At a time when most of the country was
skeptical about Carter's religious affiliations, evangelicals came out in full support
of this Democratic candidate. However, as George Marsden claims, "Despite his
evangelical credentials, Carter's liberal Democratic politics soon proved unpopular
with many evangelicals."[18] By the 1980 campaign, evangelicals, assisted and organized by the nascent Moral Majority, were ready to stand behind one candidate that
would reflect their growing concern for the Christianity of America. Ronald Reagan
proved to be that candidate. Exemplifying this trend, in the 1980 presidential debates Reagan appealed specifically to nationalistic evangelical sentiments, claiming, "I have always believed that this land was placed here between two great
oceans by some divine plan. It was placed here to be found by a special kind of
people. . . . I have found a great hunger in America for a spiritual revival, for a belief
that law must be based on higher law, for a return to tradition and values that we
once had."[19] Such rhetoric won the hearts of many American evangelicals and ce-
mented the new relationship between conservative Christians and the Republican
Party. This relationship is important both because the visibility of the Christian
Right inspired many evangelicals to actively participate in political actions, and also
because it increased the popularity and visibility of conservative Christianity within
the wider American public. Evangelical involvement in Reagan's campaign persuaded many evangelicals that Christianity had a place within the political realm.

Republican leaders in the early Reagan years encouraged the support of preacher-
politicians such as Jerry Falwell. Christian leaders brought with them votes, funding,
and the resources of dozens of organizations like the Moral Majority, the Christian
Coalition, and the 700 Club. In return for conservative Christian support, Republican
leaders met regularly with these ministers and, in many cases, took their concerns
regarding the American morality seriously. In some cases, as with evangelist Pat
Robertson, conservative Republicans even encouraged Christian leaders to run for
office themselves and supported them with advice and election plans. Robertson's
campaign for the 1988 Republican presidential nomination laid the foundation for

evangelical participation in future elections, as Operation Rescue's Randall Terry claims: "In the late 80s and early 90s, we're seeing a whole new wave of Christians come in[to politics]. . . . Rev. Pat Robertson's presidential campaign brought out of the pew and into the process tens of thousands of new people, many of whom are still involved. Their full impact will not be felt until the 1996 election, the 2000 election, 2004."[20]

The cumulative effort of political Christians throughout the decade yielded a significant number of Christians involved in party politics, as well as a widespread, grassroots network created not with the ordinary organizational tools of the Christian Right (such as direct mail and church related contacts), but rather—once again—through television. Christian television programs such as *The 700 Club* and *The Old-Time Gospel Hour* informed viewers about political candidates who would support the family values campaign, and encouraged them to back these candidates. These same viewers then turned their channel to the evening news and saw Christian political candidates professing to restore morality to America. This televised link between conservative Christianity and Republican Party politics cleared a path for many Americans to understand, accept, and support Christians in politics.

Despite these strong connections and networks, Robertson's presidential campaign failed, and by the early 1990s conservative Christians had reoriented their strategies to focus entirely on the local level. Their self-stated goal was to sponsor an affiliated Christian candidate in every local campaign across America—from city government to zoning board—by the year 2000.[21] Moreover, in conjunction with backing particular Christian candidates, the Christian Right marshaled popular support for social campaigns that enforced "traditional values." For example, the Family Protection Act (FPA), initially introduced to Congress in 1979 and reintroduced in various versions every two or three years since then, was designed "to preserve the integrity of the American family, to foster and protect the viability of American family life . . . and to promote the virtues of the family."[22] Behind these goals lay very specific ideas of what the family should be. For example, the FPA encouraged women to be full-time homemakers through a variety of tax incentives, and increased the power of parents by denying teens access to birth control without parental consent. As Seidman sees it, the FPA "was intent on preserving the heterosexual married family unit in which the wife attends primarily to domestic tasks and the husband assumes the breadwinner, head-of-household role."[23] Although the

FPA has never been passed, continuous debates over its merits and drawbacks were among the many issues keeping "the traditional family" at the forefront of American politics.

The Christian Right's turn to politics was motivated not just by the desire to protect "traditional" gender roles but by the belief that America is, as Jerry Falwell states it, "a special agent of God in the world," and by the desire to restore Christian principles as the foundation of American government. From the perspective of the Christian Right, the nation must adhere to Christian principles of morality in order to fulfill its heavenly charge. Christian, biblical, American, and conservative values are thus conflated, as is readily apparent in the Right's discourses. Randall Terry, for example, states that he hopes to transform America into a country which would "actively try to build [its] laws and institutions around the principles and laws of the word of God."[24] Pat Robertson—who names his monthly tabloid *Christian America*—claims that liberated sexuality is responsible for the downfall of America, that "the arguments of radical feminists have led to the wrath of God descending on this land that we love so much."[25] In the glossy "Faith and Freedom Calendar" Robertson mails to Christian Coalition members each December, George Washington is pictured kneeling before God at Valley Forge, and Benjamin Franklin is shown breaking a deadlock at the Constitutional Convention by calling for prayer. The calendar intentionally collapses American heritage and Christian symbolism. Similarly, James Kennedy announces, "I will say to Ted Koppel or Dan Rather or anyone, without apology, that America is worth saving and that JESUS CHRIST IS THE ONLY PERSON IN THIS WORLD WHO CAN SAVE AMERICA."[26]

Although as Noll, Hatch, and Marsden articulate, the claim that America is uniquely and exceptionally Christian carries no historical or Scriptural evidence, various components of the campaign for family values support the campaign for a Christian America.[27] Working to make the two-parent "traditional" family the norm for all Americans is part of the crusade. As Falwell states, "The family is the basic unit that God established, and its continued health is a prerequisite for our healthy, prosperous nation. No nation has ever been stronger than the families within her."[28] In the thinking of the Right, the family functions as the social unit upon which a Christian nation can be built.

The appeal to Christian nationalism strengthens the Right's myths of gender formulations, sexual morality, and the "traditional family." In the collapse of Christianity with American nationalism, everything that is American is Christian and everything that is Christian is American. Both strands beseech conservative Christians to live lives centered in sexual purity and full-time stay-at-home motherhood. As historian Randall Balmer states, the appeal to nationalism "conjures images of a halcyon past when evangelical Protestant values prevailed in American culture, when a woman tended her domain in the household and thereby ensured the spiritual welfare of her family. These mythologies, no matter how far removed from reality, energize political involvement by serving as a constant reminder of how decent and righteous America used to be."[29]

Thus, when contemporary Christians look at history through the lens of Christian nationalism, they see specific gender roles, gendered theology, and sexual purity not only in all of their Christian ancestors, but in their American foremothers and forefathers as well. In this frame, the traditional family is the way that both Americans and Christians have always organized their sexual and social lives. The impact of Christian ideology coupled with American nationalism creates an atmosphere that renders gendered theology and the image of the 1950s traditional family very difficult for most conservative Christians to resist. In the rhetoric of the Right, keeping sex confined to marriage and people organized into gender-dependent theological units is overdetermined by both religious and nationalistic historical myths, so much so that the origin of the "traditional family"—fictional television programs—is completely elided.

As Christian nationalism supports the family, the sociological existence of "traditional" families in many conservative enclaves strengthens the sense of Christian nationhood. The seemingly self-evident moral nature of "traditional" values, and the number of people conforming to them, supports the idea that the American nation must have some kind of special Christian call. The enterprise of American exceptionalism depends on conservative Christians organizing their sexual lives so that women—the gender that is actively constructed as possessing superior moral and spiritual attributes—successfully confine sexual intercourse and most other sexual encounters to romance and marriage. As this sexual ethic is held up and lived in conservative communities across the country, America itself looks more Christian. Moreover, if the self-evident moral way for people to live is—as the Right would have it—in "traditional," nuclear families, and that method of social organization is *both* Christian and American, then in the minds of conservative Christians, America must be a Christian nation and a chosen land. In this sense, gender and sexual organization construct a particular kind of nationalism among conservative Christian Americans, that of a uniquely Christian America.[30]

Thus, the project adopted by conservative Christians today has two discrete components which buttress each other: the sense that America is uniquely Christian and divinely ordained to be so; and the gendered theology, sexual purity, and traditional family campaign which is both produced by Christian nationalism and itself produces and proves that nationalism. Yet another argument backs the family values campaign: the peculiar yet powerful theology of premillennialism. Although not all conservative Christians are premillennialist, many of the movement's leaders are.[31] Millennialism in general is the belief that there will be a long period of peace and righteousness on earth, called the millennium, associated with the second coming of Christ. Postmillennialist Christians believe that Christ will return *after* the church has established the millennium through service, faithful living, and the preaching of the gospel. The goal of postmillennial Christians is to build a better world that will in turn bring on the millennium and Christ's return. Premillennialist Christians, on the other hand, believe that Christ will return before the millennium to sort out the good from the bad, the saved from the unsaved, and that it is this division (rapture) that will itself inaugurate the millennium.[32] Premillennialist Christians do not believe that their actions can save the world, so they work primarily for their own salvation.

The premillennialist belief that only God's direct intervention will bring about the reign of peace lends itself to a deep pessimism about human progress—be it national policy or sexual liberation. In this view humanity is traveling further and further from the righteous Kingdom of God. While individual people may be redeemed, history itself is doomed; its only hope is in its destruction. Yet there is a role for human action. Premillennialist Christians believe that the righteous must continually do battle with the evil forces of history in order to be chosen as one of the elect at Christ's return. In past years, this battle had been waged between the evils of science, Darwinism, and higher Biblical criticism—seen as efforts to distort or ignore God's word—on one side, and the truth of the Bible on the other. This battle continues today in the campaign for family values.

Many premillennialist narratives are explicit endorsements of American exceptionalism. In them, the evil force that must be fought is non-American, nondemocratic, and non-Christian. In these visions of the future, America is victorious over foreign nations precisely because America's people are more virtuous and family oriented. Hal Lindsey's popular *The Late Great Planet Earth*, for example, uses various biblical prophecies to pit Israel and America against the European Common Market, Russia, and Arab allies in a worldwide catastrophe whereby only faithful Christians will be raptured.[33] Similarly, Pat Robertson's *New World Order* argues that the center of power for the "New World Order" rests in Arab and Islamic leadership, which constitutes a "secret power center" that is attempting to control the American economy. (Indeed, he argues that "sodomites," secular American university professors, and Masons have already fallen under their power.) Robertson narrates an apocalypse in which the only real winners are faithful Americans who value the family.[34] Similarly, Robert Van Kampen's *The Sign* uses specific Scriptures to interpret the reunification of Germany and the collapse of the Soviet Union as signs that the Antichrist of sexual revolution is gaining international power.[35] In all of these narratives, America will be saved only if she continues to return to the full-time motherhood and sexual purity of the campaign for family values. Thus, the family values campaign is intertwined not only with the saving of America but with Christian salvation itself.

Premillennialist theology offers not only predictions about how and when God will bring the world to an end, but also prescriptions for Christians to follow to ensure that they will be among the saved when that end occurs. As one believer states, "Eschatology is a call to holiness and right living. . . . Will we as the church be motivated by the vision of God's ultimate future to be about the Lord's business in the present era until Christ comes in glory?"[36] For the Christian Right, the campaign for family values defines this call to holiness and right living. Televangelists, radio preachers, and leaders of the Christian Right such as Pat Robertson, Jerry Falwell, Kenneth Copeland, Jimmy Swaggart, James Dobson, Marlin Maddox, Rex Humbard, and Texe Marrs regularly refer to the second coming of Christ in their broadcasts and use those opportunities to suggest that those people who adhere to traditional gender formulations and conservative viewpoints about sexuality will be among the saved when the event occurs. Dr. James Kennedy boldly portrays it on his letterhead: "The world as we know it is rapidly collapsing," and uses the eschaton as his governing image to extol traditional family values.[37] Recent Christian films with titles like *A Thief in the Night, A Distant Thunder, Image of the Beast, Years of the Beast, Early Warning, The Rapture, Revelation, The Return, The Final Hour,* and *The Road to Armageddon* vividly portray the competing factions of the end times when, in every case, the "winners" are those who are associated with the traditional family values. In their desire to be identified with and included among the saved, Christians are given a political script that, these stories suggest, guarantees salvation.

The coagulation of gendered theology, sexual purity, political involvement, and salvation is visible in the Right's activities around abortion in the early 1980s, the initial project of the family values campaign. Abortion succeeded in galvanizing the fears and emotions of the Christian Right because the decision to legalize abortion both offered women increased freedom from the constraints of child rearing and the home, and called attention to the liberalization of sexuality in general. Antiabortion activism allowed people to express their discontent with the social and sexual shifts since the 1960s, and to demonstrate their commitment to the Bible and to Christian social action in a public and visible way. On one level, the activities of the pro-life movement were intended to "save babies"; on another level, the antiabortion campaign was also engineered to demonstrate that those Christians who cared enough to get involved were among the elect, that is, were "saved" themselves.

The antiabortion campaign also became a useful vehicle for promoting the conservative agenda on sex and gender. Pro-lifers learned to use the extensive national media attention their protests received to promote the broader message that intended to confine women to the home and sex to marriage. While many secularists found the "rescues" appalling, dangerous, or simply silly, many disillusioned Christians saw in the rescues a way to reinvigorate their lives with meaning. Thus, media coverage brought such Christians the message that if they were losing hope in the world, they, too, needed to respond to God's call by getting involved in politics.

The antiabortion campaign had several positive effects for the Christian Right. First, it supported sexual purity; from the perspective of the Right, the entire, unpleasant intervention could be avoided by stronger interdicts against sex outside of marriage and aggressive support of abstinence. Second, the campaign to revoke abortion rights supported the logic that dictated that a woman's highest vocation was motherhood. Both male and female pro-life champions often argue against abortion by directly appealing to Cult of Domesticity logic. For a woman to deny the maternal vocation by aborting her child is to oppose her very nature and reason for existence. Even when antiabortion rhetoric was not so clearly derived from gendered theology, it still caused many Christian women to reconsider their options and have the babies. The Right's opposition to abortion, then, in fact produced more mothers; the visibility of many Christian women performing the role of mother reified gendered notions about God, parenthood, and the family. The antiabortion campaign in effect kept women in the home, in their place, and available for theological tasks. Finally, and perhaps most importantly, the antiabortion campaign introduced the notion that political involvement is a way to salvation. Through antiabortion activity, Christian pro-lifers made themselves visible on a national level as people who cared enough about the world and its moral decay to get involved on a grassroots level. By blocking access to clinics and postponing or preventing abortions, these activists relayed a message across the country that it was time for Christians to get involved. If other Christians wanted to work toward their salvation, organizers such as Operation Rescue's Randall Terry claimed, they needed to demonstrate their righteousness by risking their careers and reputations to save the babies.

In the 1990s, the Christian Right has shifted its oppositional gaze from the issue of abortion to a practice which seems to conflict with the family values campaign even more than abortion: homosexuality. Now that I have investigated the theological rationale behind the Right's passionate defense of traditional gender roles and its opposition to nonmarital sex, the reasons for this conflict are clear. By portraying gays and lesbians as outcasts from and outsiders to the family values project, the Christian Right shores up the idea that only those on the conservative side of these family-oriented issues are saved. Gay people have become the backdrop against which the traditional family, along with saved, Christian America, defines itself.

The amount of antigay and homophobic material produced by the Christian Right is astounding. For example, nearly half of the issues of James Dobson's *Focus on the Family* magazine contain cover stories or major stories (more than one page) devoted either to attacking homosexuality or to former homosexuals who now live—happily—in "traditional" families. Similarly, of the first eight issues of Beverly LaHaye's *Family Voice* (published by Concerned Women of America), half featured major stories opposing homosexuality, including two cover stories. Every one of the first twelve issues of Pat Robertson's *Christian America* featured antigay stories. Moreover, several conservative Christian organizations exist for the sole purpose of eradicating gays and gay life from Christian America, including The Report, producer and distributor of the film *The Gay Agenda*. Dozens of Christian books with titles like *Sodom's Second Coming*, *Legislating Immorality*, and *Unnatural Affections* attack homosexuality. Public legislation sponsored by Christian politicians designed to support the traditional family almost always works also to oppress gay and lesbian people. For example, the Family Protection Act attempted to deny federal funds, including Social Security, veterans' benefits, and student loans, to any individual or private or public organization that, in any way, could be said to advocate homosexuality or present homosexuality as an acceptable lifestyle. Gay people have become a main target for the contemporary Right's crusade to define and represent what a Christian is not.

The Right's denunciation of homosexuality stems from its convictions about gender, marriage, and family life.[37] Gay people conflict with the ideology of the traditional family because they do not confine sexual activity to (state-sanctioned) marriage. Because they are not (and, for the moment, cannot be) legally married, the Right presumes that all sexually active gay men and lesbian women must be, by definition, promiscuous.[38] The AIDS epidemic is seen as proof of the immorality of their actions. As Gregg Albers states in *Plague in Our Midst: Sexuality, AIDS, and the Christian Family*, "The AIDS epidemic is a direct result of sexual immorality and promiscuity in the homosexual community. This promiscuity leads not only to AIDS but to rape, murder, and abortion as well."[39] Or, as Patrick Buchanan articulates it, "Homosexuals declared war upon traditional values and now nature is exacting its awful retribution."[40] From the Right's perspective, AIDS is yet another sign that anything that disrupts the ideology of gendered theology is immoral.

The Christian Right has used the AIDS epidemic, through two contradictory arguments, to promote two different goals. On the one hand, AIDS is seen as a gay disease, a punishment for promiscuity and immoral sexual behavior; therefore the only people who get it are those who have gay sex. As F. L. Smith portrayed it in the popular *Sodom's Second Coming*, "Less than 1 in 3500 heterosexuals get AIDS. . . . Even heterosexual sex with a partner who has AIDS is relatively safe." (Indeed, Smith goes on to suggest that all counts of reported heterosexual AIDS have occurred in Africa.) His argument implies that although heterosexual AIDS is a possibility, it is not a real problem facing straight, white people in America.[41] In a similar vein, George Grant and Mark Horne's *Legislating Morality* suggests that AIDS is undeniably "lifestyle-specific," that "AIDS is almost exclusively contained within identifiable homosexual communities."[42] Michael Fumento's *The Myth of Heterosexual AIDS* likewise portends that "infection data continue to show that infections from heterosexual transmission remain extremely low. . . . More white males are diagnosed with breast cancer each year than the number who have been diagnosed with heterosexually transmitted AIDS during the entire epidemic."[43] These lines of argument suggest that AIDS exists only in gay communities, all of which are presumed to be promiscuous. Indeed, as Spenser Hughes explains, "AIDS activists work for a cure for the disease because only a cure would allow homosexuals to return to the old, uninhibited lifestyle, the way it was before AIDS put such a deadly damper on their sexual adventuring." [44] This language makes monogamous heterosexuals feel protected from the epidemic, and renders homosexuality itself unsafe, immoral, and even deadly.

But on the other hand, factions of the Right also argue that AIDS is *not* a gay disease and that anyone—including heterosexuals—can get it. This second strategy promotes sexual purity by suggesting that the only "safe sex"—especially for heterosexuals—is abstinence. This line of argument asserts that AIDS has spread more quickly and vehemently into heterosexual populations because gay people have blocked measures to confine and control the disease. Thus, from the perspective of the Right, although purity is already the only moral Christian stance, it is made all the more necessary by "immoral, promiscuous homosexuals" who make the world unsafe. According to Stanley Monteith, to take one prominent example, thousands of heterosexual health care workers die of AIDS each year because they do not know which of their patients are infected. In his *AIDS: The Unnecessary Epidemic*, Monteith argues that "we need to start treating HIV disease like a disease rather than a civil rights issue" by requiring mandatory testing for everyone and isolating infected individuals through quarantine. Monteith argues that these public health initiatives are being blocked by the homosexual lobby which opposes such interventions because they would decimate the homosexual population:

> From the beginning of the epidemic, ACT UP and similar militant groups had used threats, confrontation and intimidation to direct the course of our nation's response to "the plague." . . . These groups have held our public health policy hostage. They have utilized the horror of the epidemic to gain their political and social objectives. Their domination of our nation's response to this epidemic has led to the unnecessary spread of the disease not only in the homosexual population, but through-out the drug-using population and now into the heterosexual population. The actions of these groups, along with the liberal media, have been effective since April of 1982 in blocking effective public health measures from being used to control the epidemic. [45]

Other commentators on the right agree with Monteith's analysis. For example, in *Plague in Our Midst*, Gregg Albers states that "epidemics can only be brought under control when reasonable means of precaution are taken to prevent their spread. . . . The political strength of gays has stopped almost all state legislation that would call for the testing of risk groups, the reporting of positive tests to public health authorities, and the tracing of all known contacts."[46] Similarly, Paul Cameron, director of the Institute for the Scientific Investigation of Sexuality, vehemently argues that the federal government has negligently acquiesced to the political demands of homosexuals. As he puts it, "We have for the first time the interesting coincidence that the people who brought the disease to our shores are also homosexuals who make a lot of noise and who have a lot of political clout. We have a politically protected virus sheltered in the bodies of people who are making a great deal of noise and getting a lot of attention."[47] And in his inimical bluntness, Jerry Falwell argues that "gays should be rounded up and quarantined like sick animals."[48]

This accusation that homosexuals have too much power in proportion to their population is prominent on the Christian Right. As Spenser Hughes contends in *The Lambda Conspiracy*: "Homosexuals are among the most affluent, well educated, and privileged people in the country . . . they have used their disproportionate political power to pressure medical officials all across the land into discarding public health measures that would control the spread of AIDS. That power has gained homosexuals virtually full legal sanction to commit acts that have caused the exponential spread of a 100 percent fatal disease for which we still have no cure."[49] Similarly, George Grant and Mark Horne argue that "gays have more money because they don't perform the social function of having children," and because they have this financial advantage, "[they] are represented positively on TV and in the movies because gays exert undue influence in Hollywood."[50] From the perspective of the Right, the cultural power that gays (allegedly) have is bad not because it represents gay liberation or gay positive social programs, but rather because such power is out of proportion to their demographic representation. That is, the Right argues that even though gays have all this power and money, there are in fact relatively few gay people in society. Although most traditional, scientific estimates and surveys suggest that ten percent of the population is gay, the Christian Right's own research argues that less than one percent of the population is gay.[51] This small percentage serves to further marginalize homosexuality in the mind of the Right, while at the same time suggesting that the gay agenda does not enjoy widespread support and could be defeated.

Gay influence is most dangerous, according to conservative commentators, in schools. F. L. Smith articulates this concern: "There are gays all across America who are discussing over coffee what would be the best way to expose your sons and daughters to the moral acceptability of a gay lifestyle."[52] In particular, members of the Christian Right allege that positive images of gay people in the classroom, including those in textbooks, will promote sexual activity among young children. Therefore, they say, schools should not purchase any books that affirm gay lifestyles (including and especially the widely publicized children's books *Daddy's Roommate* and *Heather Has Two Mommies)*. The assumption here is that representations of same-sex couples/families promote sex in a way that representations of heterosexual couples do not. As one commentator put it, "The old curriculum had no references to sex,"[53] even though that curriculum contained many representations of heterosexual families.[54]

The debates over representations of sexuality in the classroom do not end here, however. From the Right's perspective, efforts to positively represent gay people in the classroom are inextricably connected with attempts to include sex education in public school curriculums. Sex education, the Right says, is part of the gay agenda because discussing sexuality in general with adolescents will inevitably lead to homosexuality and promiscuity. "We have abandoned our own children to sexual promiscuity in the guise of helping them 'handle' their sexuality," John Ankerberg and John Weldon assert in *The Myth of Safe Sex: The Tragic Consequences of Violating God's Plan*, and that abandonment "will cause our kids to have more sexual problems like homosexuality in the long run."[55] Indeed, the Right believes that the main goal of sex education is not, as its supporters would assert, to prevent pregnancy and AIDS, but "to promote an atmosphere of acceptance of many different kinds of sexuality at very young ages."[56] In fact, sex education is not only wrong but unnecessary, because sex should be confined to marriage and not discussed until that point. As George Grant and Mark Horne argue, "Less time should be spent on sex education, because sex is something that should come only inside marriage and only with spiritual training."[57] Or, as conservative leader Connie Marshner put it, "Sex education is something that can be taught in two hours. More time only encourages bad ideas and illicit behavior."[58]

The campaign against homosexuality is not only related to the Right's opposition to nonmarital and premarital sex. Homosexuality also disrupts the Right's demand that people live in families in which the man goes out to work and the woman stays home to raise the children and care for the home. If both a man and a woman are necessary for spiritual wholeness, households set up by same-sex partners will, by such logic, have imbalanced or incomplete access to God. As Jerry Falwell explains, "Heterosexuality was created by God and is endorsed by God. We would not be having the present moral crisis regarding homosexuality if men and women accepted their proper roles as designated by God." [59]

In much of the rhetoric of the Christian Right, objections to gay men are stronger and more visible than objections to lesbian women. This disparity is at least in part related to the fact that most conservative thinkers are men who understand their maleness only within the frame of gendered theology. For them, male homosexuality is a crime not only because same-sex sex is intrinsically wrong, but also because in male-male sex, one of the partners takes up or momentarily identifies with the role of "woman" and disrupts the gendered hierarchy articulated in the last chapter. That is, although women stand for connection to God, they also, as Welter and other feminists saw in the Cult of Domesticity, stand for submissiveness, passivity, and unproductiveness. Christian Right leaders are especially concerned about anal sex, I suggest, because in that act, the man who is penetrated becomes symbolically associated with femaleness. [60] Such activity is particularly threatening when the theological frame surrounding gender depends on the separation of male qualities from female. The salvation promised by the Christian Right dictates that Christians must be *either* male or female, must exist in an identifiable "traditional family," and, of course, must be heterosexual. The Christian Right polices the boundary between gay and straight by denouncing, ridiculing, and condemning homosexuals—especially gay men—as a way of marking themselves within a stable category of heterosexuality.

In academic classrooms as well as in popular culture today, the differences between male and female and between gay and straight are being questioned; homosexuality, heterosexuality, masculinity, and femininity are beginning to be understood as socially constructed roles that rely on certain historical modes of representation and performance rather than as natural attributes of a person. On a popular level, preoccupation with cross-dressing and the breakdown of gender boundaries can be seen in the popularity of celebrities like Dennis Rodman, Michael Jackson, Madonna, and Fabio, and in films like *Tootsie* and *Mrs. Doubtfire*. At the academic level, "queer theory" challenges the idea that all people fit into only two genders, and suggests a broader range of possibilities. These academic theories are put into practice in political movements such as ACT UP, Queer Nation, and other organizations that attempt to bring about gay liberation through the destabilization of sexual categories. The recent backlash of the Christian Right corresponds in part to these initiatives.

For example, in the 1992 *The Gay Agenda in Public Education*, one conservative commentator complained that he could no longer "tell men from women." "Men are growing breasts [a reference to the visibility of transgendered people at a gay pride march], and women are taking their shirts off. You can't even tell they're women."[61] What's at stake in this comment is the need of those conservative Christians to know who and what (gender) they are, especially in relation to God. Conservative Christian men and women feel that their access to God is dependent on their gender and their sexual orientation; if the distinction between men and women or gay and straight is challenged or deteriorates, how will they know how to relate to God? Thus, the Christian Right reacts against these new cultural and academic currents by clearly defining and then condemning homosexuals. For them, a stronger and firmer category of "heterosexuality" is generated by creating, excluding, and repudiating "homosexuality." In the sexually unstable world of the 1990s, the campaign for family values targets and ostracizes homosexuality in order to render heterosexuality clear and safe.

It is worth repeating that conservative Christian homophobia stems from the desire to maintain relationship with God. From a conservative Christian perspective, homosexuality threatens relationship with God precisely because our relationship is built on the very idea that God knows us through our gender. The presence and social acceptance of homosexuality challenges the concept of a God who is known solely or primarily through gender. By their very existence, gay people—and particularly gay Christians—contest the notion that human beings are meant to live in nuclear, heterosexual families. As a result of their desire to be faithful to and known by God, conservative Christians today are producing an environment in which theological reassurance, salvation, American exceptionalism, homophobia, and political involvement have become gravely interdependent.

Feminist Christian ethicist Beverly Harrison has argued that the connection between misogyny and homophobia occurs as a result of the "problematic tendency of the Christian theological tradition to neglect, ignore, or denigrate the body."[62] She argues that things that signify sexuality or corporeality—such as women and gays— are thus thought to be less spiritual. While this anticorporeal ideology does circulate in the general tradition of church theology, it is not conservative Christianity's core objection to homosexuality. As discussed earlier, the marriage manuals of the Right demonstrate that conservatives wholeheartedly support sex in instances that uphold the overarching structure of gendered theology. Instead I believe that the connection between sexism and homophobia is much more functional. The vicious animosity directed toward homosexuals—along with other aspects of the family values campaign—keeps women at home and dependent on men and thus guarantees every Christian man, woman, and child a relationship with God. Recognition that the bifurcation is not simply between "flesh" and "spirit" brings into sharp focus how hard conservative sexual ideology and the campaign for family values work to keep women in their place.

The current struggle over homosexuality in the church, then, is not only a struggle about the morality of sexual preference; it is a conflict rooted in Christian identity and the nature of God. As F. L. Smith states, "Gay rights is not just another political issue. Nor is it just another moral issue. Gay rights presents us with the ultimate issue of our time: whether or not God will ever again be honored in our nation."[63] I suggest that it is not a question of *whether* God will be honored, but rather a question of *which* God will be honored. The struggle among contemporary Christians over the moral acceptability of homosexuality is directly related to who God is perceived to be and how we think God relates to us in the world today.

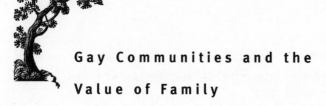

CHAPTER FOUR

Gay Communities and the Value of Family

The cornerstone issue of the gay rights movement should be the legal recognition of gay unions.

Bruce Bawer

While the Christian Right championed and developed an extensive discourse about the value of the family and the sinfulness of homosexuality, mainline Christian denominations failed to issue clear, unambiguous statements on these issues. Even progressive Christians marshaled no counterpart to conservative rhetoric. In part this is due to the fact that the belief that the heterosexual nuclear family was both superior to other configurations and in need of protection was hard to escape. It was advocated not only by religious conservatives, but also by an assortment of scholars, journalists, and cultural critics who asserted the family's superiority on sociological or psychological rather than religious grounds. For example, political theorist Jean Bethke Elshtain argues that the nuclear family was the source of values necessary for resistance to corporate power and antidemocratic tendencies in the modern world. From her perspective, the heterosexual family was the most natural way of intimately relating to other human beings and therefore ought to be encouraged for the good of democracy and the nation.[1]

In a similar fashion, many "middle-of-the-road" journalists began to champion the role of family in American culture of the early 1990s. For example, the cover of the April 1993 *Atlantic* unabashedly announced that "Dan Quayle Was Right," and the accompanying story by Barbara Dafoe Whitehead proclaimed that "the social arrangement that has proved most successful in ensuring the physical survival and promoting the social development of the child is the family unit of the biological mother and father."[2] Pro-family journalists and scholars formed a network which, as sociologist Judith Stacey describes it, "forge[d] a national 'consensus' on family values that has . . . shaped the family ideology and politics of the Clinton administration."[3] In a reversal of his earlier position, Clinton endorsed family values at the end of 1993 in his statement, "I believe this country would be a lot better off if children were born to married couples." This sentiment, along with the scholarly research and journalism that supported and produced it, created a consensus among the general American population that the nuclear, heterosexual family was the best possible social arrangement.

With national support for the family growing at such a rapid rate, many progressive and feminist Christians who fundamentally disagreed with conservative values and politics found it hard to escape the logic of the "traditional family." Some important Christian attempts to challenge the Right's attitudes toward the family inadvertently reinscribed the nuclear, heterosexual family as the only moral way of organizing social and sexual life within the church. Mary Stewart VanLeeuwan's *Gender and Grace*, to take one prominent example, opposed the Christian Right by arguing that Christians ought to see the church as their "first family." She suggests that the Right's total focus on the nuclear family undermines the strong call to communal life articulated throughout both the Old and New Testaments. As she writes, "Jesus' own life and teachings underscore the fact that marriage and family now take a back seat to the universal proclamation of God's salvation and the formation of a new 'first family'—a world-wide kingdom-building company, in which membership depends not at all on bloodlines, but on faith in the Messiah." However, VanLeeuwan went on to explain that the Christian's second family—or the household in which smaller parts of the whole reside—must be based on heterosexual sexuality because "women and men were meant to complement each other. . . . It is not just that human beings need other people in general; they need a sense of female/male complementariness to be complete and to image God fully."[4] Although VanLeeuwan made a strong case for the acceptability of celibacy within the church, and attempted to advocate a Christian community larger than the family, for those who want to be sexually active the only acceptable mode is heterosexual intercourse within marriage and family.

In a similar vein, Rebecca Groothuis's *Women Caught in the Conflict* criticizes the discourse of family values for "denying women the kinds of opportunities for leadership and equality that women now enjoy elsewhere in society." She rejects the gender roles associated with conservative Christianity in favor of a "biblically based feminism" whose goal, in her words, is that "men and women be allowed to serve God as individuals, according to their own unique gifts rather than according to a culturally predetermined personality slot called 'Christian manhood' or 'Christian womanhood.' . . . the goal of biblical feminism is that men and women in the church might be liberated from the preoccupation with power and authority that characterizes the traditionalist agenda, so that everyone may serve God freely and whole-heartedly without the anxiety that one might be stepping out of one's place in the 'chain of command.'"[5] Although her critique of theological gender roles is strong, it does not extend into the realm of sexuality. For Groothuis, men and women ought to enjoy the mutuality portrayed in the Scriptures, except when it comes to sexual intercourse, in which, she claims, men and women have divinely ordained roles. She argues that women must be submissive to their husbands within the nuclear, mo-nogamous marriage; "evangelical feminism" encourages women to challenge the roles associated with gendered theology, but simultaneously requires women to participate only in heterosexual, nuclear families at home. Although many Chris-tians like Groothuis attempted to resist the conservatism of the Right, most fell into the trap set by the logic of the Cult of Domesticity. Because they could not imagine salvation existing in a social and sexual order other than the nuclear, heterosexual family, they could only endorse that family as the model of Christian living.

Perhaps the most surprising conversions to family rhetoric occurred among gay men and women that sought both to raise children and to "marry" in publicly recognized unions at astonishing rates from the early 1980s on. Although many gay people have chosen to live in monogamous, committed relationships, often with children, for many decades, it wasn't until the 1980s that gay people en masse sought the protection and acceptance accorded heterosexual nuclear families. In state and lo-cal initiatives all over the country, gays and lesbians fought political battles to be-come foster parents, to adopt children, to gain domestic partnership rights, and to have gay families be recognized as families for purposes of insurance, social secu-rity benefits, and immigration. New works such as Kath Weston's *Families We Choose: Lesbians, Gays, Kinship*; Laura Benkov's *Reinventing the Family: The Emerging Story of Lesbian and Gay Parents*; and Phyllis Burke's *Family Values: A Lesbian Mother Fights for Her Son* chronicle the gay and lesbian quest for family, and represent these quests as the natural extension of gay liberation.[6] The position of gay families in the wider campaign for family values is complicated. It is sufficient here to say that on some level, these interventions, and the families they represent, seek legitimacy for gays and lesbians by showing that lesbians and gay men form families—including families with children.

Mainline and progressive Christians have a difficult time responding to this wide-spread valorization of family. On the one hand, many of our churches either openly or tacitly endorse the value of the heterosexual nuclear family. Church life, more often than not, operates around the assumption that every member is part of a functioning biological family; there are worship services and social programs for children, husbands, wives, fathers, and mothers, but rarely for lesbian or gay partners. On the other hand, however, the kinds of families advocated in today's traditionalist discourses make it very difficult for many Christian women to seek vocational fulfillment outside the home. It is virtually impossible for any woman to juggle the traditional religious expectations that exist for her inside the home with a desire for a career outside it. As we saw in chapter 2, traditional domestic ideology does offer benefits for women, including the opportunity to cultivate spiritual attributes and wield religious authority. But the "traditional family" model also deprives women of economic and social power.[7] Thus, while most progressive Christians do not accept the extremely rigid gender roles prescribed in the Right's family values campaign, they do accept heterosexuality and heterosexual marriage as the norm.

Several theologians have suggested that this tacit acceptance of heterosexuality is based neither in Scripture nor in long-standing Christian tradition, and in doing so, they have successfully challenged the root of the family values campaign. In his *Families at the Crossroads*, Rodney Clapp demonstrates that these gender roles prescribed for today's families are not based on a Scriptural model. The Bible, he claims, has no concept of public or private and thus no gender roles corresponding to these competing domains. He writes, "Israelites simply did not divide the private and public worlds, as does the [nuclear] vision of the family. Ancient Israel had no centralized, industrial economy, so households provided their own economic wherewithal . . . Neither father nor mother left the 'private' world to go earn the family's bread in the 'public.' " The idea that the mother was responsible for her family's spiritual life was foreign to the lives of people represented in the Bible; as in preindustrial America, men and women in ancient Israel worked side by side to produce both material and religious life. Moreover, Clapp claims that "the family" in Hebrew culture was radically different from the traditionalist conception. In his words, "the average American household consists of 2.63 people. The average Hebrew household numbered closer to 50 or 100 people." Hebrew families were large multigenerational units, an arrangement which made daily life easier and more efficient in an agricultural economy. Finally, Clapp notes that notions of romance and sentimentality so prevalent in contemporary discourse about the traditional family were virtually absent from Hebrew culture. Although affectionate bonds might have existed between a man and wife, they were not necessary for the marriage to be considered valid and good. In Hebrew culture, marriage represented a covenant not merely between two individuals, but between two families; as Clapp writes, "In short, marriages were arranged—usually by the fathers—to consolidate the strength and resources of the families involved."[8]

While Clapp does not recommend that Christians go so far as to take up the practice of arranged marriages, he is highly critical of the sentimentality associated with contemporary traditional families. He argues that this sentimentality means that family issues are often not taken seriously in public culture. He claims that "the family has been stripped of its wider and public significance and left only with intimacy and 'private' relationships as its purpose."[9] Thus, even though the religious Right has accrued political power as a result of its campaign for family values, the family itself is a weak, sentimentalized institution. Thus, when spirituality and Christian training are confined to the private sphere of home they, too, are often trivialized or compromised along with the domestic sphere. Indeed, this is precisely Janet Fishburn's concern with contemporary family rhetoric. From her perspective, the contemporary family values campaign is problematic largely because it advocates that the work of spiritual instruction and moral formation should be done by the family. That is, in the rhetoric of family values, the wife and mother is better equipped than any institution to train her children to be good citizens and good Christians. Fishburn argues that as a result of this interpretation of family, churches no longer do the work of Christian training; Sunday schools and other religious education are haphazard and low-priority activities for most churches. The nuclear family, in Fishburn's evaluation, actually does a disservice to the institutional church by substituting the family for the work of the church.

Both Clapp and Fishburn argue for a more community-based approach to Christian life. For both, the current focus on the family allows the institution of family to replace the church. According to both, Christians are called to understand the church as our primary community; our emotional and social obligations ought to occur with other Christians, whether or not they are part of biological or legal family. The family, they argue, takes our focus off of our Christian duties. As Fishburn expresses it, "[We] have not been able to sustain a legitimate critique of poverty and injustice in America because the family ideals of the American Dream continue to be linked to democratic values and economic stability. Uncritical loyalty to the family makes it very difficult to see or comprehend the plight of the poor and homeless, the oppression of minority persons, as anything but their own fault. To ask middle-class Americans to see American culture as Jesus would see it is to ask them to vote against their own privileged position in society."[10] Fishburn astutely points out that although family values rhetoric benefits many of us, it stands in deep conflict with Christian understandings of self and service to neighbor. While neither Clapp nor Fishburn addresses the issue of homosexuality directly, their insights can serve as a place to begin the reconstruction of sexual ethics.

I agree that as Christians, our primary social and emotional obligations and relations ought to rest not on biology but rather on baptism. Even a cursory look at Christian history reminds us that much of our tradition is devoted to helping us live more connected, communal lives. From Saint Benedict to Dorothy Day, from the Anabaptists to the Oneida experiment to the Shakers, Christian leaders and movements have challenged those commitments that take primacy over our church communities, including our allegiance to family. The church has historically attempted to break down the boundaries that exist around primary, particular relationships in favor of relationships and dependencies on a community of believers. Christians throughout the centuries have understood that life in Christ means being responsible to and for many more people than one's spouse and children. Life in Christ, in the most radical sense, demands an openness to other community members.

Thus, the bifurcated gender roles associated with traditional family values produce a social fabric not only in which one's relationship with God is predicated on one's gender, but also one in which these "traditional families" themselves usurp the place of Christian community. As an increasing number of Christians live in a way that is responsible only to their immediate family members, we lose the ability to be the church. The campaign for family values draws us away from living connected, community-based Christian lives to a more isolated and separated form of living. Moreover, as Christian salvation becomes more and more attached to traditional family values it simultaneously becomes detached from its communal heritage. Because we live in an age where complying with traditional family structures is enough to guarantee salvation, we are losing sight of the richness that communal living can produce. In short, we are losing our ability to imagine the radical nature of the Body of Christ.

Gay-affirming Christian theologians do not escape this valorization of family over community. In many recent works, the goodness of a gay relationship is measured by its resemblance to the nuclear family. Several new works in Roman Catholic pro-portionalist reasoning demonstrate this deep commitment to the family by arguing that while heterosexual intimacy and procreativity are the ultimate goods of sexual intercourse, stable and monogamous homosexual unions—which at least provide the end of intimacy—are better than "unstable, promiscuous" sexual practices that might otherwise result. Moral theologians Philip Keane and Vincent Genovesi, S.J., argue that if the option of the celibate life is not available to some homosexuals, it is better for those homosexuals to be involved in loving, monogamous relationships rather than promiscuous, lascivious sexual encounters.[11] Thus, in these works, cer-tain monogamous homosexual unions can be understood as moral, not because they are inherently good, but rather because their goodness stems from the fact that they are best alternative available.[12]

Another Christian justification of homosexuality rests on the idea that homosexual activity is no less moral than intentionally nonprocreative heterosexual activity; that is, homosexuality is morally equivalent to the use of birth control. In this rea-soning, both birth control and homosexuality can be understood as procreative in a wider sense as a pledge or assurance that if a new life were to be brought to the relationship both partners would welcome and support it together.[13] Thus, for example, Patricia Beattie Jung and Ralph Smith, in *Heterosexism: An Ethical Chal-lenge*, argue that the objections to homosexuality based on procreation are not suc-cessful because "we [Christians] do not consider heterosexual couples who marry but remain childless less married than others who procreate" and further because "homosexual couples can procreate with the assistance of a third party."[14] Jung and Smith argue that committed, monogamous same-sex relationships can be as moral as heterosexual unions. Indeed, they argue that discriminatory attitudes toward same-sex unions are themselves sinful.

In each of these texts, support of same-sex activity is made possible by a condemna-tion of sex outside of committed, monogamous relationships. That is, "the family" need not be heterosexual, but it must be nuclear. For the proportionalists, homosex-uality inside a monogamous relationship is permitted precisely so that homosexuals will not be forced to act out their sexual desires in secretive, promiscuous, non-committed settings. A committed gay relationship achieves the good of unity while avoiding the evil of promiscuity and licentiousness. For Jung and Smith, the ends of unitivity and procreativity—whether gay or straight—can only happen in commit-ted, monogamous relationships "because all human beings must learn how to love

each other [and] such schooling takes time, effort and patience. . . . Fidelity understood as permanence is a practical requirement necessitated by our need to learn
how to love one another." For Jung and Smith, promiscuity is immoral "not because it
breaks a specific promise, but because everyone is short changed in the process." [15]

The position that accepts homosexuality only in the case of committed, monogamous relationships is not at all uncommon. Popular Episcopal Bishop John Shelby
Spong, for example, tells us that "the relationship in which sex is shared needs to be
exclusive. . . . Multiple sex partners at the same time is a violation of vulnerability,
commitment, honesty, and the reality of caring." [16] Similarly, Sidney Callahan supports monogamy as the only moral option for gays because, as she puts it, "two persons can become united as one in a way that is impossible for three or four persons. . . . The symmetry of a monogamous dyad," she explains, "works toward the
equality of those in the relationship because there must be constant give and take
in a bounded unit, particularly if it continues over time." [17] Indeed, when gay people
today seek refuge in Reconciling, Open and Affirming, Reconciled in Christ, and
More Light congregations, [18] the church expects them to be either single (and pre-
sumably celibate), or involved in a monogamous and permanent relationship. The
most progressive of our churches today will bless a same-sex union in a noncivil ceremony, and thus reinforce the idea that it is acceptable to be gay only inside an exclusive relationship.

The writings of several theologians attempt to complicate this straightforward endorsement of heterosexuality by supporting the possibility of nonmonogamous relationships in the ideal. They argue that although nonmonogamy is difficult to execute in daily life, it should not be prohibited abstractly. Works by ethicists J. Michael
Clark, Carter Heyward, James Nelson, and Mary Hunt do not endorse monogamy as
a good end in itself, but rather as a means to the good of a faithful relationship. As
Clark represents it, monogamy is "a pragmatic and mutually chosen means for nurturing the most healthy and wholistic sexuality-in-relation for two people committed to a common process of growth and liberation together." [19] In each of these
works, monogamy is understood as the most practical and most viable way for gays
and lesbians to exist in today's world. Thus, although these ethicists entertain the
possibility that a person can sustain more than one loving relationship in theory,
their model for the ideal relationship in practice remains nuclear, isolated, and
heterosexual.

Even this tacit emphasis on monogamy urges gays to mimic heterosexual relational structures. Our allegiances and commitments, like those of others, must belong not to the larger community but to our partner or nuclear family. We are encouraged to participate in the American dream by buying a house and living "together," that is, to separate ourselves from larger kinship systems. While living in our nuclear units, we will necessarily buy and use more than we would if we were part of a larger support community; we are urged, in short, to be good consumers. If consumption fails to keep us entertained, we are prodded to reproduce like heterosexuals, that is, to "have" our "own" biological children through new reproductive technologies. When two adults and one or two children live together in an isolated fashion, the person who makes the most money will most likely decide where the unit will go and one member of the couple can easily become dependent on the other's greater income. Gay people today have become experts at impersonating straight nuclear families; the only thing that is different is that one of us is the wrong gender.

The urban cultures of gay men and other radical sex communities offer a different model. In *The Culture of Desire*, Frank Browning reports that "by the spring of 1991, New York, L.A., and San Francisco had seen the proliferation of the revived sexual underground. . . . Open rooms in the warehouses of depleted industrial zones [appeared], where in the small hours of the morning, young men lined up with their buddies to probe, caress, and gnaw at one another's flesh in dimly lit tangles of animal abandon."[20] These activities, often described as "anonymous," "promiscuous," or "nonrelational" sex, have been widely criticized as dangerous, immature, or immoral by many liberal-minded Christians. These practices are seen as the product of a particular kind of masculine psychology that is driven by a base and insatiable sexual desire and which consequently cannot commit to "the real thing," that is, to monogamous relationship. I suggest to the contrary that many gay and radical sex communities are composed not of people who have failed to meet the "universal" standard of exclusive relationship, but rather of people who have organized their sexual-social lives on a different model, a model that is fundamentally communal. In many of these worlds, allegiance to the entire community is often more vital and meaningful than any particular coupling within that community. The practices and attitudes generated by these people can help shed light on what communal living might mean and how it might function.

In America today, even in the age of AIDS, dozens of young men leave the small towns and heartlands every day and make their way to urban centers because they have come to believe that a community awaits them there. Sometimes they come only after reading about Castro Street in a magazine they once found left in a bathroom; other times they come having memorized the entire map of New York City, knowing where every gay bar is on that map. Often they are innocent young men who are driven by a desire to find a world where they will be accepted and honored, where they can belong without hiding a part of themselves, where *their* dreams, too, can come true. When they get there, they may well find a community of men who will remember what it is like to be young and alone and scared and broke. They will find men who believe, as Paul Monette writes, that "it's a kind of duty to the tribe to take care of [these kids] and make it all less frightening."[21] The fortunate ones will be initiated into the social fabric of that community not only through sex, but through crashes courses in taste and style. There they will learn to renarrate their lives in the frame of homosexuality, to see themselves as always having belonged. They will stake out emotional territory inside the lives of other men, and feel responsible even for those friends with whom they have not shared sex, for they recognize in this community that each is part of the other. Moreover, this pattern is not limited to the practices of gay men (although it is historically more prevalent in gay male communities). Lesbians, bisexuals, and heterosexual men and women increasingly find themselves attracted to a growing number of sex-based communities, where sharing sex in the larger community is the signification of membership.[22]

The many works of fiction, memoir, and academic study stemming from and/or commenting on gay urban and radical sex cultures often feature a scene in which, for example, a young man finds his first sex in a bathroom or bar and emerges from that space changed for the better. As sociologist Steven Seidman reports, "Casual sex [is] viewed as a primary community building force in gay life. Through casual sex, gay men were said to experience heightened feelings of brotherhood and male solidarity. . . . Barriers of age, class, education and sometimes race were said to be weakened as individuals circulated in this system of sexual exchange; competition and rivalry between men might give ways to bonds of affection and kinship."[23] Though not all gay communities operate in this utopic fashion, in some, each sexual encounter shores up membership in the community and each person's participation makes the community he finds stronger for others. Although he may not know the names of each of his sex partners, each encounter resignifies his belonging. And although no member of the community makes steadfast promises to any one person in the community, each in his own way promises himself as part of this world. Intimacy and faithfulness in sex are played out on the community rather than individual level.

This culture gay men and sex radicals inhabit sometimes challenges racial or class prejudices. As Browning put it, "The parks and the bathhouses have been places of freedom and fraternity . . . places where the cares and duties of the day dissolved, where barriers of class and education might temporarily evaporate." [24] There is a sense in which the men in the parks and bathrooms and bars have no separate identity, no history, no background except that of belonging to this community. Everything else about them, where they come from, what they do, is eclipsed by their identity as gay men. These communities function and grow even in the AIDS crisis. The virus threatens each and every person; everyone who goes to a bar or backroom to share sex—whether male or female, gay or straight—is vulnerable. And yet they continue to come. They leave behind high school diplomas, families who love them, college educations, chances of advancement, all to be part of this world. AIDS hasn't stopped these communities; indeed, it has only made them stronger.

I suggest that what happens in many gay male cultures and radical sex communities is not anonymous, promiscuous, or nonrelational sex, but "communal." Sex in these worlds is not anonymous because that would mean that the partner is somehow unknown, and as one gay male friend of mine put it, "Even though I may not know his name, I know what music he listens to, what food he likes, where he vacations. His name is incidental. He's part of our world, that's all I need to know." Similarly, sex in these enclaves is far from promiscuous or indiscriminate because partners are chosen precisely because they belong inside that community, and because they show physical signs (such as taste in clothes, food, music) of participating in that world. Finally, sex in these communities is completely relational in that it functions as a way of inscribing members into an identity larger than oneself. Rather than condemning these communities, other Christians ought to pause and think about what we could learn from a group of people who base their social and emotional existence on such a communal model.

Of course, not all gay communities fulfill this potential. Gay communities can be merely locations of sexual acting out, places where one goes only to avoid intimacy.

J. Michael Clark, for example, calls them "ghettos" and argues that such activities "institutionalized patterns of behavior that prevented ... any possibility of intimacy. 'Glory holes,'" he continues,

> *which revealed not persons but only penises, utterly blocked relational intimacy; darkened, music-filled bathhouses and orgy rooms likewise presented only vague bodily forms in fog and steam, while they precluded intimate communication and reduced the human participants again to merely genital machines; even the seemingly more personal one-night stands with bargoing "tricks" were generally begun under the veil of dim lights, loud music, and alcoholic haze, consummated often enough without so much as an exchange of names, and, after orgasm, cleaned up and cleaned out of one's life as quickly as possible, lest the post-coital awkwardness give way ... to any undesired intimacy.* [25]

Other critics of the gay subculture argue that readily available sex dissuades men from seeking monogamous, long-term relationships. Bruce Bawer, for example, believes that promiscuity is an ineffective and spineless response to the fact that gay people are not allowed to marry; he argues that it is simply easier for gay men to stay in the closet and lead promiscuous, secretive lives than to face society with a visible, permanent partner. He accuses gay men of giving into carnal desire and argues that it is precisely promiscuity which prevents gay Americans from claiming their "place at the table." [26] Others, such as Larry Kramer, find that many aspects of these communities are grounded in a landscape where lying, cheating, and adultery are normative, where men make monogamous commitments and break them, where promiscuity is simply a way of avoiding intimacy with one's partner. [27]

But rather than writing off gay communal sex as immoral, I believe it is important to investigate the positive, communal aspects of gay and radical sex cultures because these communities are one of the few remaining places where the hegemony of the heterosexist, capitalist, patriarchal, nuclear family is challenged. To reproduce the structure of that family with same-sex couples is to reproduce a system founded on oppression. The church needs the model of gay sexual communities because Christians have forgotten how to think about social and sexual life outside the family. In America today, because being Christian is generally socially acceptable and without risk, we do not depend on the support of other parishioners in a way that makes us part of them. We remain separate, individuated Christians, tearing down the walls of our selves only with our husband or wife, only within the fortress of the family, only with one, monogamous other. Indeed, the family has become the master issue for the Christian Right precisely because those Christians have lost their ability to be dependent and interconnected, because they have lost their ability to be church. The ideological handle that the Right holds onto most dearly—the family—is the very thing that prevents them from being church. Likewise, the thing they most critique about gay life—"promiscuity"—is the very practice of caring for one another and the stranger that they themselves have forgotten.

As Christians, we ought to attempt to understand the gay model of community as a challenge to the isolation that pervades society today, an isolation that is all too familiar in our churches. The hegemony of the nuclear family renders those living outside this structure alone; even within the families, loneliness abounds. We are not responding as the Body of Christ when such isolation occurs. Indeed, as Philip Turner notes, "An issue far deeper than sexual ethics confronts us. It is the absence of a community of Christians in which no one need be alone. The deep issue is not sex but the constitution of the church."[28] Gay men can teach us how to be responsible to a community wider than just our partner and children. The communal lifestyle that they enact shows us how to become a deeper part of one another's lives.

Commitments to monogamy run deep, however, and when gay men and lesbian women seek community with Christianity today, they are most often granted membership only on the condition of monogamy. Thus, many left-leaning, liberal, or radical Christians today argue in favor of gay marriage or commitment ceremonies within the church so that lesbians and gay men can take part in church life. In order to become a part of the church, many gay people abandon communal sex practices to fulfill the expectations placed on them by the Christian community.

I believe this strategy is misguided. Gay Christians must instead look beyond the currently popular political struggle for recognition of same-sex unions and gay families, into a landscape where the heart of sexual morality is constituted not by membership in a nuclear family but rather by what is pleasing to God. By allowing the main or primary issue of gay activism in the church to be the blessing of same-sex unions, we obscure the complicated sexual lives of many gay people, particularly those who live their lives in more complex communities. Perhaps even more importantly, by focusing our attention on the family, we lose sight of the central role that our church communities ought to be playing in our lives. As Christians—both gay and straight alike—we need to learn how to live in a way that is more focused on and intertwined with specific church communities. Many of our gay brothers lead such enmeshed lives in their own gay subcultures. Rather than condemn their life-style or demand that they organize themselves into monogamous families, I suggest that we attempt to learn from them just how rich communal living can be.

The Right's family values campaign has gained ground by promoting an idealized view of the family as a haven in a heartless world. These conservative Christians rightly understand that the Christian message is designed for a unit larger than one individual, that morality and faithfulness can only be achieved in a group setting. In their focus on the family, they appeal to those of us who feel isolated and de-tached from larger units. The family provides contemporary Americans with a tool for overcoming the crippling and lonely effects of individuality. The Right's campaign tells us that we are not alone as long as we have a family. I suggest that we gay Christians also need to work to disrupt the self-contained, isolated human sub-ject—but by advocating deeper dependencies and connections, not with biologi-cal family members, but with those we call church. The Right alleviates loneliness with blood ties; faithful Christians ought to assuage the pain of detachment with baptism.

The question, then, is where left and progressive—and particularly gay—Christians ought stand in relation to the concept of the family. Should we accept the family as the dominant modality of morality or should we understand morality as something that exists independent of medium (that is, the family *can* be a good but it's not the only acceptable way to live)? Should we fight for legal acceptance of gay families or focus on allowing a space for more communal orientations?

Several recent studies on homosexuality and family life indicate that an increasing number of gay and lesbian people are following the former strategy. Each year more and more couples publicly pledge commitment. Each year more lesbians and gay men become families by producing or adopting children. The pro-family gay dis-course accompanying these efforts tells us that the legalization of domestic part-nership and the subsequent sanctioning of gay families is the way to end discrimi-nation. The family has become the vehicle, it would seem, for gays to fit in to society, to blend into the heterosexual landscape, to be accepted. As Gabriel Rotello writes, "Gay marriage is what most individual lesbians and gay men across America want. And they want it because it's consonant with a main goal of liberation: to drop stigma from homosexuality, to make it socially equivalent to heterosexuality."[29]

And yet, when these ethnographies are read closely, the families of gay people look quite a bit different than the family valorized in Christian Right rhetoric. Where the conservative Christian family consists of a married couple and their biological children, the gay "families" depicted in works such as Kath Weston's *Families We Choose* and Laura Benkov's *Reinventing the Family* come in all sorts of configurations, from a committed lesbian or gay man raising a child alone, to more complicated arrangements that might include the sperm donors, surrogate mothers, ex-lovers, and nonbiological parents. Where the conservative Christian family strives to close itself off from outside influences, often shunning even the involvement of grandparents or non-nuclear relatives, gay families are usually open to the involvement of many different kinds of relationships. It is not uncommon for the children of gay people to have two mommies (a biological mother and her partner), and two daddies (a biological father and his partner) and numerous aunts, uncles, and others who are related to the child not by blood but by choice. Indeed, when pro-family gay materials are examined carefully, it is often the case that the gay family—even when the couple is sexually monogamous—is more communally oriented than its conservative Christian counterpart.

Indeed, I suggest that what gay people mean by *families* is very different than what conservatives mean by the term. Far from an acceptance of the narrower definitions promulgated by the Right, the appeal to family is a way of recovering the term for a progressive communal project. As Laura Benkov writes,

> Lesbians and gay men challenge "family values" rhetoric by expanding the definition of family—emphasizing relational aspects like love and commitment over any particular family structure. We challenge the myth that places lesbians and gay men on the side opposing children and families. And in reclaiming our relations to family life, we assert our humanity in the face of dehumanizing forces. Remapping the territory that constitutes the family is, thus, a critical part of the work we need to do. But in doing this work it is important that we not buy into the fetishism of family—the idea that participation in family life, above all else, defines one's morality and that family relationships are paramount.[30]

Benkov suggests that we can use the rhetoric of family without falling into the traps set by the Right; we can live in kinship units called "families" without adhering to the Right's definition of what constitutes such a group. In short, she suggests that we can live in families without participating in the pro-family ideology.

As a gay Christian, I do not believe the family will save us, either in the political sense that it will render homosexuality socially equivalent to heterosexuality or in the sense of Christian salvation. The current gay pro-family agenda is problematic, because even though the ethnographic data and illustrations are filled with examples of communal living, the argument that these kinship networks are *families* and therefore are *legitimate* feeds into the logic which valorizes family life as the only acceptable means of social organization. As Christians we cannot dismiss the value of any social organization that challenges the hegemony of the nuclear family, for in understanding how others construct viable communal lives we move closer to restoring ourselves to the Body of Christ.

The family is one way of organizing social life which neither guarantees nor prevents morality in sexual relationships. Many families are good places to grow up in and be part of, but many others are not. Those of us who have had positive experiences with communal living, whether in convents, monasteries, intentional Christian communities, or in gay and lesbian "subcultures," know that it can be moral, vibrant, and life giving. We need a way of discussing sexual morality that does not hold up heterosexual marriage as the *only* ideal. We need a moral language that will help us understand the depth and intensity of our intimate connections without demanding that we fill our needs only within the heterosexually prescribed, dominant pattern. In short, we need the church, along with its heretofore homophobic tradition of moral inquiry, to think clearly about the role of sexuality in our lives. As I will show fully in chapter 6, the moral markers of unitivity and procreativity can be applied to every sexual relationship—gay, straight, monogamous, or communal—to give us a way of distinguishing good sex from bad.

Secular arguments in favor of gay marriage often frame the issue as one of privacy; heterosexuals ought to tolerate same-sex couplings because what we do at home is our own business. But this argument is not appropriate within the church. The church challenges the distinction between the public and private, between the personal and the political. As Christians we are called to reveal ourselves to one another in order to become part of one another, in order, finally, to participate in the Body of Christ. We want a church that offers guidelines for thinking about when sex is good and when it is bad, and then celebrates with us, for us, when we create and sustain sexual relationships that achieve those moral goals. These relationships may be inside something that we call "family," or they may be inside a group of people who have dedicated themselves to each other in another pattern. Either way, Christians should refuse to be sequestered into the invisible space of "privacy," just as we refuse to be morally defined by the discourse of family values. What we need to ask each other is this: Is the sex we're having pleasing to God? If it is, then our relationships should be proclaimed moral and celebrated throughout every church.

I am not claiming that the connection between sex (gay or straight) and morality is in any way "natural," but rather that the Christian tradition has historically understood sexuality as involving both the church and God. Those of us who call ourselves Christians live in a world where sex has come to mean something not unlike "Holy Communion." Although the idea that sex has this meaning has been used by patriarchal and homophobic regimes to limit and regulate sexual behavior, abandoning traditional associations is not our best option. Rather, we must strive to recapture the moral definitions of unitivity and procreativity to encompass those sexual practices that have united us with each other and with God and that we re-create openly and daily for younger generations of gays and lesbians to enter. We are all, I believe, trying to escape meaninglessness in our lives. We do not want to look back at our ties to other people as an empty waste of time. We want to escape the hurt that accompanies not belonging anywhere. Some of us do this with people of the same sex, others with people of the opposite sex. Some of us do this by having long-term, monogamous relationships, others by living in communities where love and support and belonging exist in different patterns. In any case, the pertinent question is not which kind of partner or pattern is the only ethical one, but rather which kinds of sexual interventions change our lives and make us part of one another, which acts unite us into one body, which contexts fight meaninglessness. These questions, which lie at the heart of the moral tradition, ought to constitute the heart of gay activism in the church as well.

The lines that need to be policed, then, are not the ones between monogamous and communal sex, but rather those between good and bad sex. While marriage and monogamous coupling are not inherently bad, they are not inherently good either. And while some lesbians and gay men might choose monogamy (and therefore should have both legal and ecclesial access to marriage), other Christians—both gay and straight—might choose to live in communities where they share sex. In all of these arrangements, we need to talk about what it means to please God with our sexuality; we need to investigate methods of opening ourselves to receive the soul of another; we need to discern what spiritual gifts we need to have in order to keep ourselves vulnerable and open to the other; we need to think about when power operates inappropriately, unethically, in a sexual encounter.

This, of course, will not be easy. Conventional interpretations teach us to make rules about abstractions: sex inside a marriage without birth control is moral, sex outside marriage is immoral. As long as we are within the boundaries, we never have to think about whether or not our own souls are open, desirable, or even wanting. As Rowan Williams writes regarding these conversations, "The question of human meaning is not raised, we are not helped to see what part sexuality plays in our learning to become human with one another, to enter the body's grace, because all we need to know is that sexual activity is licensed in one context and in no other." [31] A Christian evaluation of sexuality will return to the heart of the moral tradition by examining concrete practices in context rather than accepting hollow dictums on abstract acts and identities. The moral tradition can help us understand communal sex as a legitimate Christian practice which every Christian could endorse. It is not the only appropriate means of sexual expression, of course, but it is one of many ways that Christians can express commitment, connection, and interdependence. When sex acts, whether gay or straight, monogamous or communal, function in ways that lead us to God, they ought to be considered moral. The family does not guarantee such moral status, and indeed sometimes prevents us from fully participating in the community of church.

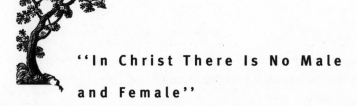

CHAPTER FIVE

"In Christ There Is No Male and Female"

The Social Construction of Gender and Sexual Identities

It is not sexuality which haunts society, but society which haunts the body's sexuality. The social body precedes the sexual body.

David Halperin

Even more than gay marriages, the most hotly debated and contested policy issue in mainline Protestantism today may be the ordination of homosexuals. Since 1990, many denominations have launched large-scale studies of homosexuality with major attention to the issue of gay ordination. The results have been confused and contradictory on whether or not gay people are welcome in the ministry. For example, the Episcopal Church's current official position, generated at the 1979 sixty-sixth General Convention and affirmed in 1991 at the seventieth General Convention, recommends that although homosexuals may be ordained, they must remain celibate after their ordination. As the document argues, "It is not appropriate for this Church to ordain a practicing homosexual, or any person who is engaged in heterosexual relations outside of marriage."[1] That is, the absence of gay marriage is used to explain why "practicing" homosexuals ought not be ordained.

The Presbyterian Church (U.S.A.)'s 1991 report "Keeping Body and Soul Together: Sexuality, Spirituality, and Social Justice," took a different tack, arguing that "ordination to church office be open to all members of the Presbyterian Church (U.S.A.), regardless of their sexual orientation and that celibacy not be a requirement for ordination."[2] But the report was defeated later that same year; although denominational leaders called for further study, they affirmed the idea that practicing homosexuals should not be ordained. In the same vein, while the United Methodist Church's 1993 "Report of the Committee to Study Homosexuality to the General Council on Ministries" carefully and exhaustively affirmed the individual worth of homosexual persons especially in pastoral settings, it ultimately refused ordination to the "self-avowed practicing homosexual."[3] Finally, the 1993 Evangelical Lutheran Church in America's study "The Church and Human Sexuality: A Lutheran Perspective" attempted to recommend "more openness on the part of the church toward

gay and lesbian persons" while at the same time affirming earlier Lutheran positions suggesting that "homosexuality is a departure from the biblical, heterosexual
structure of God's creation."[4]

These denominational documents and teachings have set a confused tone for mainline American Christians, endorsing at best a "don't ask, don't tell" atmosphere,
and at worst a sense of grave instability regarding Christian social teaching. Our
confusion is largely due to the fact that these official denominational positions are
attempting to satisfy both conservative and liberal factions within the denominations. This is no easy task, because both advocates for gays and lesbians and their
opponents argue that their position is the only one compatible with the heart of the
Christian message. From one perspective, official endorsement of gays to the ordained ministry would be a stroke of liberation; from another, it would only be a ca-
pitulation to social pressure to condone morally corrupt behavior. The current
church documents reflect the attempt by mainline denominations to adjudicate between these two deeply opposed beliefs. As a result, if gay ordination is allowed at
all, it is contingent on invisibility. Gay Christians who hope to serve the church
through ordained ministry need to be able to "pass"—in the eyes of the church—as
heterosexual; although individuals may identify themselves as "gay," they are not
allowed to act, to seem, or to "practice" in any way differently than heterosexual
Christians.

As these conflicts and the resulting inconsistent official positions demonstrate,
mainline denominations are no longer speaking or acting as unified bodies, but
rather as a group of divergent and competing factions. American Christianity is no
longer united under a coherent or comprehensive set of religious symbols, or by beliefs about the role of religion in public life, the authority of the Bible, or the eschato-
logical vision behind the new creation. We are instead divided, as Robert Wuthnow
has observed, roughly into two competing political orientations: the liberal church,
which holds that inclusivity, tolerance, and social justice lie at the heart of the Christian message, and the conservative church, which valorizes tradition and family-
centered values as the core of Christianity.[5] The conflicted denominational positions on homosexuality, then, reflect the fact that each denomination is filled with
Christians of both liberal and conservative persuasion. While some mainline denominations—such as the Southern Baptist Convention—lean more to the right,
and others—such as Quakers and the United Church of Christ—lean more to the left,
the majority of mainline denominations fall in the center and include both liberal

and conservative members. The denominational social teachings, because they are attempting to mediate between two very incommensurate factions within the denomination, offer quite conflicted maps for any gay person pondering ordination.

While I am fully persuaded that our churches are politically divided as Wuthnow describes, I will show that the competing factions of the debate over the ordination of homosexuals actually share virtually the same set of underlying premises regarding the nature and history of homosexuality. As Mary McClintock-Fulkerson suggests, "What is so striking about the terms of the ecclesiastical debate [on homosexuality] is not the differences between the opposing positions . . . but the assumptions shared by those who would have an inclusive church and those who would not."[6] By examining the limitations of the presuppositions shared by both liberal and conservative mainliners, I will suggest a Christian position on gay ordination that escapes the polarized logic of contemporary debates and ultimately offers a more coherent and faithful understanding of homosexuality to American Christians.

The opposing sides involved in denominational debates, along with the scholarly research supporting their competing assertions, make a number of assumptions worth investigating. First, most liberals and conservatives agree on the idea that homosexuality is self-evident; we all know exactly what homosexuality is and can identify it both in today's milieu and throughout history. The work of John Boswell, widely acknowledged as authoritative in denominational conversations, serves as an example here. In his highly influential *Christianity, Social Tolerance, and Homosexuality*, Boswell argues that gay people have a recoverable, positive history and a direct lineage with gays who lived within the early Christian Church.[7] According to Boswell, the Bible says relatively little about homosexuality because it was a fully accepted part of everyday life; people who self-identified as homosexual were completely integrated in early Christian culture. The few passages in Scripture and in early patristic documents that oppose homosexuality were, according to Boswell, either written by people who were from rural areas where homosexuality was much less common, or were written about individuals with heterosexual orientations who opposed their own natures by participating in homosexual acts. While this conclusion is debated among mainline Protestants, Boswell's assumption that homosexuality as we know it existed in the ancient world is virtually uncontested.

For example, Richard Hays accepts that homosexuality existed in the ancient world and argues that the Bible is much less friendly toward gay practices and people than we are today.[8] For Hays, the practices, meanings, and intentions associated with homosexuality have gone unchanged for 2,000 years and hold the same ontological and ethical status in the ancient world as they ought to today; that is, in his condemnations of "acts against nature," Hays argues that Paul was referring to the same acts that we know today as homosexuality. In a similar vein, Richard John Neuhaus argues that Boswell's favorable reading of Scripture is misleading; "Christianity has, in a clear and sustained manner," he claims, "always taught that homosexual acts are morally wrong."[9] Thus, like Hays, Neuhaus assumes that what counts as homosexuality looks, feels, and *is* the same across time and culture.

Paired with this shared assumption that homosexuality is transhistorical and transcultural is the shared belief that homosexuality is the result of some biological or natural phenomenon, that some people are simply born homosexual.[10] What remains in the debate, therefore, is whether it is acceptable or moral to act on those natural desires. As liberals see it, the naturalness of homosexuality indicates that homosexuality is part of God's design and therefore that gay men and lesbians ought to be free to act on their desires. Indeed, many suggest that homosexual desire, like heterosexual desire, is a gift from God and ought to be embraced and celebrated. Because, as one Methodist states, "no compassionate God would demand the impossible," homosexual activity can be endorsed and practicing homosexuals should be allowed full access to ordination.[11] From the liberal perspective, responsible homosexual practice can be considered a healthy part of the Christian life, and gay and lesbian persons should be acknowledged as full participants within Christian communities.

The conservatives involved in the mainline denominational debates generally agree not just that homosexuality is biologically determined, but also that homosexual persons possess sacred worth and deserve compassion and Christian love.[12] However, because they believe that homosexual activity is a sin, conservative mainliners can only support and ordain "nonpracticing" homosexuals, that is, homosexuals who do not have same-sex sex. For them, the fact that homosexuality is a function of biology does not automatically mean that it is a good gift from God. As one Methodist explained, "There are tendencies in all of us that are to be resisted, not affirmed or followed. A predisposition toward certain thought or action does not mean it is a good gift or morally correct. Many persons are predisposed to promiscuity, immaturity, gambling, alcoholism, or a long list of other temptations. The Christian faith offers not only the motivation but the divine power to resist what is contrary to God's intention for human behavior." [13]

Thus, though homosexuals are born with a heavy burden indeed, it is not in the church's interest to lighten that burden by condoning immoral practices. Homosexual Christians can only be full participants in Christian communities—and given access to ordination—if they agree not to act on their sexual feelings. As another Methodist commentator says, "No one is barred from the ministry because of predisposition or tendency. But persons who chose to practice what the church does not condone disqualify themselves." [14] Thus, although liberal and conservative mainline Christians are politically opposed on whether or not homosexuals ought to be allowed to act on their desires, they commonly share the basic presupposition that homosexual desire is involuntary, naturally or biologically determined, and permanently stable.

A new body of scholarship challenges these assumptions. "Queer theory" and "queer history" interpret sexual behavior as a set of activities that is embedded in, and receives its meaning from, concrete and local histories and cultures. For queer theorists, homosexuality (or for that matter heterosexuality) does not exist in a transhistorical, transcultural, or natural frame. That is, rather than assuming we know what homosexuality is or which particular physical acts define every instance of it, queer theorists begin by asking what sexual practices look like and mean in different historical and cultural contexts, and move from there to greater understandings of the many ways that sexuality can be defined and expressed. The results of their inquiries can help us resolve the deadlock between liberals and conservatives in our denominational settings. In questioning the very grounds that support the current conflict, queer theory can help us find new ways to think about faithfulness in the Christian life.

In his study of the sexual practices of ancient Greece, David Halperin found that the set of practices we commonly refer to as homosexuality during that period actually looks quite different from what we know as homosexuality today. For Greek men, Halperin explains, sex was not tied to love or emotional commitment but was rather a way of representing oneself in the political order. In ancient Greece, he argues, there was no single perception of "the sex act." Instead all acts which we would call "sexual" were organized into two categories: active (meaning to insert one's penis into another's anus or vagina) and passive (meaning to receive another's penis into one's anus or vagina). The active person signified his superior place in the political realm through this act of sex; likewise, the passive partner affirmed his or her inferior status through the event. Sex was not about expressing an intimate relationship between these two people but rather functioned as a way of marking individuals in a political order. As Halperin writes,

> Sex effectively divides, classifies, and distributes its participants into two distinct and radically opposed categories. What a citizen does in bed reflects the differential in status that distinguishes him from his sexual partner: the citizen's superior prestige and authority are expressed in his power to initiate a sexual act, his right to obtain pleasure from it, and his assumption of an insertive rather than receptive role. Far from being interpreted as an expression of commonality, as a sign of some shared sexual status or identity, sex between social superior and social inferior was a miniature drama of polarization which served to measure and define social distance between them. To assimilate both the senior and junior partner in a paederastic relationship to the same "homosexuality" would have struck a classical Athenian as no less bizarre than to classify a burglar as an "active criminal," his victim as a "passive criminal," and the two of them alike as partners in crime: burglary—like sex, as the Greeks understood it—is after all a non-relational act.[15]

Moreover, in Halperin's understanding of ancient Greece, the gender of the passive sexual partner was not a fact worthy of notice. A male citizen might have chosen either a woman or a man as his passive partner, but there was no expectation that he would choose either a man or a woman every time. There is no sense in which a given citizen "was" homosexual because there was no cultural strategy to distinguish sexually passive men from women. As Halperin writes, "Sexual partners came in two significantly different kinds—not male and female but 'active' and 'passive.'"[16] Whether a man's object choice was male or female was of little consequence as long as the chosen person understood herself or himself as passive.

In what sense, then, can the sex that occurred between an active man and a passive man in ancient Greece be considered comparable to male homosexual acts as we understand them today? The diverse sexual practices which are today united under the sign of "homosexuality" have nothing to do with an individual's status in state politics. (In fact, from most contemporary perspectives, sexuality is or ought to remain in the private realm, out of the jurisdiction of any state or government.) In to-

day's setting, a man who indiscriminately selected both female and male sex partners would probably be classified as bisexual rather than homosexual. Why call the
ancient Greek practices "homosexuality" when the same set of practices today
would be categorized differently? Moreover, while some instances of contemporary
gay sex might physically resemble the practice of men-with-men in ancient Greece,
many more gay relationships are attentive to the sexual pleasures and needs of
both partners. When the distinction between active and passive is removed or
downplayed, what makes today's homosexual acts the same as those in the ancient
world? An increasing number of contemporary gay men refuse to participate in pen-
etrative sex as a result of the AIDS crisis; in what sense are they "like" their "homosexual" brothers in ancient Greece? Finally, what of lesbian women? Are they only
"homosexual" when they use a prosthetic device to penetrate their partners like ancient Greeks did? In what sense does the concept "homosexuality" identify com-
monalities among all these people and describe practices that are thought to be
morally or ontologically similar?

Ancient Greece is only one example of the innumerable array of cultures that have
constructed sexuality in a manner radically different from our own. In his study of
nineteenth-century New York City, historian George Chauncey has found another re-
markable example of such differences in the sexual practices and identifications
that existed among working-class men. According to Chauncey, in the 1880s "a third
sex" of men emerged that came to be known as "fairies." These men identified
themselves as different by dressing as women and soliciting sex with more "masculine" men. As Chauncey narrates,

> The fundamental division of male sexual actors in much of turn-of-the-century
> working-class thought was not between heterosexual and homosexual men,
> but between conventionally masculine males, who were regarded as men, and
> effeminate males, known as fairies or pansies, who were regarded as virtual
> women, or, more precisely, as members of a "third sex" that combined elements
> of the male and female. The heterosexual-homosexual binarism that governs
> our thinking about sexuality today did not yet constitute the common sense of
> working-class sexual ideology.[17]

Chauncey demonstrates that the fairy—consistent with his identification as a
woman—took the passive role in sex. As in ancient Greece, women could be substi-
tuted for fairies and fairies for women in the framework of most masculine males;
the determining factor involved in one's choice of sexual partners was not his or her

genitals but rather his or her identification as passive. Unlike today's concept of homosexuality, which focuses solely on the narrower issue of sexual object choice, masculine men in nineteenth-century New York chose both women and passive men as their sexual partners; the point was not the biological choice but preferences regarding certain roles and activities during the event of sex.

Chauncey's research shows that, while the fairy was marked as radically different in that society, masculine men—even when engaging in what we would call "homosexual acts"—were considered normal and were thought to be responding in an utterly normal manner to the radically different fairy. As Chauncey describes it,

> *The most striking difference between the dominant sexual culture of the early twentieth century and that of our own era is the degree to which the earlier culture permitted men to engage in sexual relations with other men, often on a regular basis, without requiring them to regard themselves—or to be regarded by others—as gay.... The centrality of the fairy to the popular representation of sexual abnormality allowed other men to engage in casual sexual relations with other men, with boys, and, above all, with the fairies themselves without imagining that they themselves were abnormal. Many men alternated between male and female sexual partners without believing that interest in one precluded interest in the other, or that their occasional recourse to male sexual partners, in particular, indicated an abnormal "homosexual" or even "bisexual" disposition, for they neither understood nor organized their sexual practices along a hetero-homosexual axis.*[18]

Chauncey also chronicles the later transition from the New York world of fairies and men to the world of homosexuals and heterosexuals. His work shows us that homosexuality as we know it today—in which a person expresses a seemingly natural desire for sex with other persons of the same gender regardless of dress, cultural codings, or roles assumed during the sex act—emerged only out of a complex, uneven process, marked by substantial class and ethnic differences. These queer histories, which investigate differences among sexual practices, help us recognize how relatively new, and culturally contingent, our own sexual codings are.

The concept of a sexual orientation that transcends any particular sexual script and focuses solely on the gender of one's sexual partner emerged in America at the end of the nineteenth century as a result of several material and philosophical shifts. Industrialization made it possible for a large number of people to live independently of extended family life. For the first time in U.S. history, large groups of people were able to move off the family farm, work and live by themselves in cities, and have disposable incomes which could be used to seek pleasure. The emerging concept of homosexuality as an inherent, biological, natural preference made it possible for people to identify and group together—under the nascent rubric of identity—themselves and others who might be said to have common interests, cognate desires, and similar natures. Thus, erotic communities were transformed by the discourse of sexual preference, a discourse that ascribed "identity"—either homosexual or heterosexual—to every individual based on the gender of their object choice. As Eve Sedgwick recounts: "What was new from the turn of the century was the world-mapping by which every given person, just as he or she was necessarily assignable to a male or female gender, was now considered necessarily assignable as well to a homo- or a hetero-sexuality, a binarized identity that was full of implications for even the ostensibly least sexual aspects of personal existence. It was this new development that left no space in the culture exempt from the potent homo/heterosexual definition."[19] While scholarship about the history and evolution of the sexual identity system in this period is still developing, it seems indisputable that our "transhistorical," "natural" ideas about homosexuality are only about one hundred years old.[20]

Queer theorists remind us that the categories we use to code people gay or straight are uniquely contemporary constructions. Sedgwick captures the arbitrary nature with which the twentieth century fixated on object choice as the grounding factor of sexual identity:

> It is a rather amazing fact that, of the very many dimensions along which the genital activity of one person can be differentiated from that of another (dimensions that include preference for certain acts, certain zones or sensations, certain physical types, a certain frequency, certain symbolic investments, certain relations of age or power, a certain species, a certain number of participants, etc. etc. etc.), precisely one, the gender of the object choice, emerged from the turn of the century, and has remained, as the dimension denoted by the now ubiquitous category of "sexual orientation." This is not a development that would have been foreseen from the viewpoint of the fin de siècle itself, where a rich stew of male algolagnia, child-love, and autoeroticism, to mention no more of its components, seemed to have as indicative a relation as did homosexuality to the whole, obsessively entertained problematic of sexual "perversion" or, more broadly, "decadence."[21]

Thus, it is only because we live in a culture that divides gay and straight (and uses one category to define the other) that we see certain historical practices as "gay" even though the people who participated in those practices would not have recognized themselves in such terms. In the debate that occurs in most denominational settings, pro-gay and antigay factions argue over the acceptance of gay people in biblical and other eras. However, in assuming that gay people—as we know them today—have always existed, both sides lock the debate into categories that have had meaning for only one century. To use the categories of homosexuality and heterosexuality to understand the construction of sexuality in any past era is to ignore the reality that sexualities and their meanings are produced within specific cultural contexts. To transhistoricize today's categories is to force the people portrayed in the Bible (or any other period) into the very categories that have created the phenomenon of homosexual oppression for us today.

Queer theorists thus question the usefulness of the categories "gay" and "straight" not only because they are historically inaccurate, but also because they create the possibility of oppression. In classifying one group of people (based solely on the genitals of their sexual partners) as straight and one group as gay, we run the risk of having the straight people (who are usually in the majority) understand themselves as more "normal" than, or morally superior to, the gays (who are usually in the minority). Indeed, this is the case in America today. Even when our intent is to alleviate oppression, intellectual work that assumes that the differences in sexual object-choice are fundamental or necessary distinctions will always end up with two kinds of people—gay and straight—and gay people usually will not be the empowered majority.

Why is the category of homosexuality so pervasive in American minds, and what exactly does it mean? What makes all homosexuals alike in any concrete way? Are we able to give a firm definition of a "homosexual" that would hold up in every case? What about two men who live together who don't have sex with each other? Or a man who is happily married to a woman but has sex with other men occasionally on the side? Or men who have sex with other men only while they're in prison and no women are available? Or men who have sex only in front of (but never touching) other men? Or men who have sex with other men only via phone or computer? And what precisely makes the act of men having sex with men even remotely like the act of women having sex with women? Why is the gender of my sexual partner so interesting it deserves its own (transhistorical, naturalized) category?

Indeed, many theorists today note the limitations of "gay identity" for a liberating politic. While we are allowed, in some settings, to "come out of the closet" by revealing the gender of our object choice, the discourse effectively silences us about a myriad of other preferences, connections, events, unifications, and separations that give us identity and meaning. As Ed Cohen writes, "By predicating 'our' affinity upon the assertion of a common 'sexuality,' we tacitly agree to leave unexplored any contradictions which undermine the coherence we desire from the imagined certainty of an unassailable commonality."[22] The category of homosexuality functions to evoke an imagined community; to say that I have something in common with other gay people is to assume that the object choice of my sexual desire (which assumes I recognize a solid, natural, and consistent choice in myself) is important enough to my being and everyday life that it alone can serve as a basis of commonality and identity. For many of us, this is not the case.

Mainline denominations, of course, did not come up with the idea of solidifying, naturalizing, and transhistoricizing the concept of homosexuality all on their own. Early gay liberation movements from the 1960s and 1970s also invoked these concepts as a way of claiming their place in the world, as a strategy of resistance to discourses and therapies that demanded that they change, become "normal," become heterosexual.[23] Early liberationists interpreted the sexual underground and erotic communities that flourished during the first half of the twentieth century into a natural and transhistorical "gay identity" as a political way of making alternative practices visible. People came "out of the closet" in droves in an attempt to make a space for difference in the way America organized sexuality; they represented to themselves and others the concept that married life in the suburbs was not the only road to happiness. Indeed, the concept of a firm and immutable gay identity remains an efficacious strategy against those who which believe that all homosexuals not only can, but must, change their sexual orientation to heterosexual.

Unlike mainstream conservatives, Christians associated with the far Right (as opposed to mainline denominations) today hold no ideas of a natural, transhistorical concept of homosexuality; indeed, homosexuality in their view is a new phenomenon that has both been caused by and contributed to the so-called moral deterioration of the nation.[24] Thus, the new Christian Right works hard attempting to convert gay people to heterosexual lifestyles. Through dozens of workshops and videos and hundreds of books, how-to manuals, and pamphlets, the far Right consistently portrays the message that gay people can change. Local organizations and "ex-gay

ministries" such as Desert Stream, Exodus, and His Heart, sponsor twelve-step programs and support groups for helping individuals "come out of gay lifestyle" and
"re-enter God's kingdom on earth."[25] The printed material that supports these
"ministries" portrays homosexuality as the result of sin and/or an impure heart and
suggests that the homosexual can change with God's help and love. For example,
Jerry Arterburn's *How Will I Tell My Mother?* suggests that parents of young boys
"discourage girlish behaviors," "seek counseling if he has been labeled a sissy,"
and "clarify Scriptural mandates"; if these fail and young boys "seek out a lifestyle
of sodomy," families should "refuse to speak to those boys until they take the
pledge to go straight."[26] Other books, such as Bob Davies and Lori Rentzel's *Coming Out of Homosexuality*, suggest that gay people need to "have an intimate relationship with Christ to be transformed by his grace."[27] In light of these strategies
which require heterosexuality as a precondition of Christianity, the mainline presupposition that "gay people are born that way" seems not only progressive but down-
right liberating.

Indeed, I am convinced that part of the reason the mainline denominations invoke
the concept of "homosexual identity" is to combat the hazardous conservative notion that anybody can decide to be straight. However, even though the strategy is
intended to be liberating, using "gay identity" as the ground for liberation ultimately serves to marginalize those of us referred to as gay. We might gain access to
denominational ordination, we might someday even be granted the right to marry
our partners; however, within this system of logic we will still and always be gay,
different, and therefore not the norm. Our access to ordination or marriage or mili-
tary service or the university professoriate will be granted to us at the discretion
of the people who occupy the position of normal, who can revoke access at any
time. A transhistorical, natural concept of homosexuality is effective in fighting the
dangerous ideologies of the far Right; but, in the quest to counter its violent and
abusive ideas, we must be careful not to reinstall a comparably deleterious system
in its place.

Queer theory suggests a different way. Queer theorists argue that we do not "naturally" fit in the categories of gay or straight, but are made to do so by an ideology
that allows only two concrete, stable identities to exist. These theorists suggest that
we ought to work to end oppression by living and writing from locations beyond
or outside of the current bifurcated options. They prod us to question our attachment to the stable categories "gay" and "straight," to challenge the dichotomiza-

tion of identity into only two sexual identities, and to consider a broader range of possibilities.

As Christians, we are called by God to identify ourselves as the people of God. We are *in* this world, but not *of* this world; we diligently and consciously must challenge those worldly categories that do not help us lead more faithful lives. We are taught to disregard the things that divide us, to include in our midst outcasts, tax collectors, prostitutes, people with whom—under any other set of normal or worldly circumstances—we would hold nothing in common. Through our baptism we become new people, with a new and radically different ontology; everything that we think and see and do in the world should reflect that we are a part of the Body of Christ. What holds Christians together is not wealth or class status or human-made law or ethnic background or race or nationality, but rather God's self, which is revealed to us through our membership in the Christian Church. Our primary identification is and ought to be Christian; any identification that takes precedence over our baptism is to be avoided. Thus, if we are all functioning as Christians and attempting to be faithful to the kinds of people God has called us to be, why do we need the categories of gay and straight to conduct business in our churches? To divide each other up in those terms is to accept the definitions the world places on us; it is to participate in the notion that every one of us has an inherent orientation that affects even the most unsexual aspects of our life and work. To ask whether gay people ought to be ordained is to assume that the gender of one's sexual partner affects how one participates in and conducts God's ministry. It does not. The only characteristic pertinent to ordination is Christian faithfulness.

This is not to say that Christians should not talk about or recognize issues around sexuality. Indeed, that is precisely what we need to *start* doing. In the current climate where interest and debate focus almost exclusively on "homosexuality," we make the mistake of assuming that all Christians know how to identify and participate in moral sex. Rather than spending our energies worrying about whether or not to ordain gays, we need to think more seriously about what moral sex looks like and how we can help other Christians recognize and participate in it. That is, we should be teaching teenage girls who want to be accepted among their peers how to say "no" when sex feels wrong; we should be teaching teenage boys how to mark their adulthood with other practices besides sexual conquest; we should protest advertising campaigns that use the promise of sex to sell everything from toothpaste to tires; we should be teaching young couples how to feel close to one another without necessarily being sexual; and we should be teaching other couples how to stay open and vulnerable in a relationship so that moral sex can occur. Most importantly, we should be thinking about what God has to do with our sexual practices. We should be showing each other that sex is one of many ways to overcome the loneliness of twentieth-century individuality, one of many ways to participate in the Body of Christ. As I will demonstrate in the next chapter, our discussions could focus on the differences between good sex and bad, on when and how sex is both unitive and procreative, a discussion that would allow us to talk not about "homosexuals" as an abstract category of analysis but about practices that are or are not moral.

At the end of chapter 3, I demonstrated how Christian conservatives used the concept of "homosexuality" to construct an understanding of their own salvation; I suggested there that heterosexual identity is dependent on homosexual identity. When gay activists and other supporters of gay people in the church retain a solid conceptualization of "self-avowed practicing homosexuals," we perpetuate a category that helps the Right construct and solidify its oppositional identity. As long as we gay people function to show them what they are not, the central foundation of the Right's ruinous theology remains unchallenged. I suggest that instead of playing into the needs of the Right by asking if homosexuals should be ordained, a more useful strategy for progressive politics in the church would begin not with the distinction between homosexuality and heterosexuality, and certainly not with the further divisive distinction between nonpracticing homosexuals and practicing homosexuals, but with the differences between moral and immoral sex. By relocating Christian faithfulness along the ancient lines of unitive and procreative practices rather than on the recent lines of sexual identity, all Christians—conservative, mainline, and radical—will be invited to rethink their own sexual behaviors in ways that attend more seriously to the spirit of God.

This proposal may well be threatening to those Christians who believe that their homosexuality *is* natural, and who base their political activism in or out of church on that belief.[28] I do not intend here to question the experience of these people but to invent additional ways of thinking about and marking ourselves which can attend to other important aspects of our existence. The current system not only dictates that every one of us be classified as either homosexual or heterosexual, it also dualistically requires us to understand that classification as either predetermined or a matter of individual choice. We do not ask whether other aspects of our personalities—such as whether or not we like to eat candy, fly kites, or go to the movies—

are functions of our free will or are determined by natural, biological realities largely because those aspects of our lives are not deemed primary, significant, important parts of our identity. Why should the gender of our sexual partners differ in such a dramatic way? Furthermore, when we Christians use only the categories of heterosexuality and homosexuality to gauge sexual morality, we neglect to discuss the moral issues as they relate to God; the homo/hetero binary does not allow us to think about where, when, how often to have sex and what frame of mind and spirit we must be in for the sex to be considered moral. It only prescribes what physiological equipment our partner should have; it never tells us what having sex has to do with loving God.

The homo/hetero system presumes as well that everyone has either an obvious penis or vagina, that every person has an uncomplicated, positive relationship to that organ, and that owning that piece of equipment necessarily correlates to "who we really are." The categories of homosexual and heterosexual are themselves built on the assumption that everyone is either male or female and that that gender identification is itself self-evident to all observers. But another major aspect of the queer project shows that maleness and femaleness are also socially constructed and often exist on a very unstable background, as shown below, of assumptions and fantasies about both "men" and "women."[29] Just as we cannot use the natural, transhistorical concept of homosexuality to combat the oppressions that accompany the particular categorization of "homosexual," queer theorists argue that we can no longer appeal to the transhistorical concepts of "woman" or "woman's essential nature" as a grounding for contemporary feminism, for to do so is to assume the validity of the very idea that creates the oppression in the first place. As Judith Butler writes, "An uncritical appeal to the system which constructs gender for the emancipation of 'women' will clearly be self-defeating."[30]

Queer theorists point out that there are no foolproof scientific tests for gender; there is no hormonal, chromosomal, or anatomical test that in every case guarantees that the subject being tested is either a man or a woman.[31] If gender is not simply a matter of chromosomes, genes, genitals, or hormones, then it can only be produced by a wide variety of social events, strategies, and fantasies: who makes more money, who wears a dress, who relates to God. Like homosexuality or heterosexuality, being a "man" or "woman" are our only two options; these identifications, queer theorists argue, are constructed not by biological or natural "facts," but by a culture that constantly and consistently places us in one category rather than the other. Gender (and particularly the idea that there can only be two of them), then, is also a matter of social construction. Whether one acts as male or female is a matter of performance—that is, doing the things a woman or man does and thereby coding ourselves as such—not ontological certainty. Gender is established through a culture that teaches even young children to identify themselves and behave as either a boy or girl. Like sexuality, queer theorists argue, it is something we (as part of culture) "do," not something we "are."

This theory also suggests a political strategy for overcoming gender-based discrimination. Fighting women's oppression as a separate event involving "women only" both misses the complexities of oppression and assumes and posits the very category that itself perpetuates injustice. As counterintuitive as it might seem, queer theorists propose that the lines be drawn not between women and men but rather between those who espouse progressive politics, especially around the issues of sexuality, and those who advocate "family values." They advocate publicizing the multiplicity of genders that already exist—such as in the self-presentation of trans-gendered people—in order to disrupt the binary which keeps us locked into the hierarchical man/woman system, and to remind us that gender, as well as sexual preference, are performances rather than a biological facts. Without a binary system of gender, in the new queer world, we could experience neither sexism (how could we know what a woman is?) nor homophobia (how could we imagine partners of the "same sex" if there were an unlimited number of options?). I believe that these theoretical observations could be decisively helpful for contemporary Christian politics.

If, as I have suggested above, our primary identification as Christians ought to be "Christian," why then do we need even the categories of male and female as further codings? Although it might be argued that we need to be able to identify each other as "male" and "female" in order to bear children, we Christians are called to question our attachments to biology in order to more fully receive all Christians into our church families. Christianity has historically reproduced itself not primarily through procreation but through conversion. Therefore, it should not matter in the least whether two Christian sexual partners can biologically reproduce. As long as they are willing to invite all unwanted people to their table and embrace all outsiders in their church, they should be understood as fulfilling the Christian commandment to procreate. In such a web of hospitality, surely "gender" is not the most interesting thing that can be said about each member. With the help of queer theory, we Christians could understand ourselves as a people uniquely called to hospitality. Such an identity would mirror our desire to love God by reminding us constantly that our very identity is built on welcoming, loving, and sharing the good news of salvation with others.

This Christian identity, which takes primacy over and even overshadows identities of gender and sexual preference, certainly is not going to occur on the denominational level or even on the level of the local church any time soon. We Christians use various constructions of gender to establish particular relationships with God; giving up gender identity is a frightening prospect for many of us, in part because it threatens our gender-bound spiritual lives. Attempts to live beyond gender and sexual preference can happen at first only on a very local level. We can set up intentional Christian households and small communities of worship which are dedicated to developing their Christian identity at the expense of other, superfluous identities. These communities could challenge the sexism and homophobia buried deep within all of us by diligently asking what gender and sexual categories have to do with Christian faithfulness. These communities would regularly wed people (that we used to understand as being) of the "same gender" (as well as people of "different genders") without hesitation. Their revolutionary politics would not be rooted in these actions, however, but in their capacity to look beyond such distinctions to a world where Christian faithfulness was the primary and only measure. These groups could revisit the Christian tradition in order to develop new strategies for measuring morality. We could strengthen our faith by the way we transcend gender and sexual classifications, by the way that we correlate sexual activity with spirituality, by the way we embody Paul's prescription of Galatians 3:28: "In Christ there is no male and female." Such communities, I believe, would serve as a beacon of light for those who feel oppressed by the way our churches today correlate gender roles and spirituality.

The ideology of the mid-nineteenth century was one in which women were granted the ability to commune spiritually and morally with God. Men, no longer needing to concentrate on spiritual work, could expend their energies seeking material success in the public sphere. Churches today in which men and women take up different roles in the service of the community have inadvertently inherited that nineteenth-century ideology. Even in more progressive congregations today, men are often largely responsible for keeping up the grounds, handling finances, and other tasks associated with the public sphere. Women, conversely, are mostly responsible for preparing food, educating children, caretaking and visitation of the sick, and for other activities usually relegated to the private sphere. Although these gender roles are being challenged in many places, a feeling that gender does have something to do with how we serve God often lingers. Those spiritual communities that attempt to live beyond gender could help us more fully understand the limitations associated with this kind of ideology. They could help us see how much more full of God our lives could be if we didn't use gender categories to circumscribe our possibilities.

The path is not, however, without its dangers. Understanding gender and sexual preference as socially constructed sometimes inadvertently functions as yet another cover for sexism and male dominance. That is, the desire to break open the dichotomy between men and women has often led to the valorization of those things previously associated with the male sphere. Rather than challenging the division of the world into those two, narrow categories, secular queer theory has sometimes simply eliminated or ridiculed many of the attributes associated with women. To be queer in the secular world, then, often means to be public, hard, aggressive, "in-your-face." This new discourse often dismisses attributes such as relationality, caretaking, and spirituality as accommodationist or undesirable.

The current controversy over the history and content of the category "lesbian" will help demonstrate this point. Pre-queer, "woman-identified" feminist historians and writers such as Lillian Faderman, Carroll Smith-Rosenberg, and Adrienne Rich had earlier theorized lesbian experience in the same-sex bonding among women of earlier times. Smith-Rosenberg, for example, considered as lesbians early nineteenth-century middle-class American women who shared deep emotional bonds with other women friends—bonds which, as she demonstrated, conveyed erotic, sensual feeling. She came to this conclusion even though the category "lesbian" did not exist for them to name themselves as such, and little evidence can be found that these women participated in acts of genital sex (at least as we define them today). These women were quintessential middle-class Victorians, attending to the moral and spiritual needs of their families and using their "special natures" as opportunities to form intense emotional bonds with other women. These female bonds, as Smith-Rosenberg described them, very often took primacy over a woman's bond with her husband. For a whole generation of feminist scholars, women who wrote love letters to other women were unquestionably lesbians; to name them as such meant not only to claim historical foremothers, but also to recognize, for ourselves, that the category of lesbian was larger than what we did in bed.[32]

But in the 1990s, a new generation of scholars informed by and participating in anti-essentializing queer discourses criticized these earlier feminist scholars for ascribing lesbianism to the women they studied. They noted that today's conception of homosexuality is historically unique, and that little commonality exists between our construction of "lesbian" and a nineteenth-century woman who had some sort of "special friendship" with another woman. In fact, they charged that by using the emotional bonds that existed between middle-class women as the foundation for understanding lesbianism, the earlier feminist historians had virtually ignored the working-class women who, at the turn of the century, began to organize themselves into erotic communities based on butch-fem aesthetics. As Elizabeth Kennedy and Madeline Davis articulate it, for example, the earlier scholars "give minimal attention to the explicitly sexual lesbian communities of the turn of the century, treating their [butch-fem] identities as problematic."[33] The new generation of queer scholars favors these working-class butch-fem lesbian histories and thus retheorizes lesbianism on the axis of sexual activity rather than emotionality. They downplay the "female worlds of love and ritual" and make more visible the "self-defined mannish lesbian" as well as her "lipstick-lesbian" fem partner.[34] Lesbianism, in these new discourses, is understood as a multitude of performances around both gender and sexuality, performances that have no correlation to emotionality or domesticity. Lesbianism is no longer defined by spiritual connection or caretaking but rather by public, sexual roles.

What is at stake in this controversy over lesbian history is a disagreement not only over what should count as "lesbian" sexuality but also whether those aspects of emotionality associated with nineteenth-century Victorian womanhood are traits political progressives should valorize and retain, or critique and dismiss. Underlying the early feminist narratives is the impulse to recover the passioned spiritual and emotional complexities found in the lives of Victorian women, highlighting those dimensions of femaleness as markers for feminism today. Conversely, the narratives of the new queer studies discredit and disavow those notions of womanhood as repressive and asexual; holding up instead women's ability to break out of the prison of domesticity and to identify themselves as explicitly sexual in the public sphere.

While I do not want to support the imposition of the category "lesbian" in a period in which the concept would have had no meaning, I am deeply concerned about the fact that contemporary queer narratives virtually dismiss the domesticity, emotionality, and spirituality associated with the private sphere in favor of the dynamism, development, and aggression of the public sphere. I oppose secular queer theory on this point not because it deconstructs gender, but because it often tacitly assumes that liberation is synonymous with participation in a narrowly defined "public" life. In their focus on frank discussions of sexuality—which I fully applaud— these new queer discourses have virtually eliminated the need for religion, God, and spiritual connection. The early feminists articulated a sense of sexuality (or at least sensuality) that was intrinsically tied to (what was thought to be) women's spiritual nature. In rejecting that notion of womanhood, queer theorists have thrown out also the need or desire for any understanding of God.

Sustained attention to the activities associated with the private realm is important because these tasks reproduce daily life for most human beings. The cooking, the cleaning, the washing, the child care, the errands, the gift buying, and the grocery shopping must be done in order for people to continue with the more public life of work and politics. Somebody has to do these things, and if they are not done by queers, they will be done by women. And if some "women" manage to get out of these tasks by identifying themselves as queer, then the work will be done by women of color and other disenfranchised people who cannot afford the luxury of an identity like queer. The social reproduction of daily life is hard work, and our culture has consistently passed those "unwanted," unglamorous jobs off to minorities (paying them very little) and women (and not paying them at all.) Queer theory's valorization of the public and political parts of life and dismissal of the tasks associated with the home often lead not only to sexism, but to racism and the exploitation of the working classes as well.

As a result of the fact that women have historically been connected to the home and to the jobs associated with the social reproduction of everyday life, many women— and especially many feminists—have developed a tempered style of political organizing in the public sphere. It is worth pointing out that the aggressive, in-your-face style of organizing associated with queer theory is historically associated with and largely sustained by men. After all—the queer narrative goes—gay men have had more access to material resources and to channels of political power. Why not make use of those assets in the current struggle? Thus, the popular wisdom of the new queer coalitions holds that the beings we used to call "women" have become much better political organizers as a result of their affiliation with those beings we used to call "men." An excerpt from Sarah Schulman's *My American History* illustrates this point. "Pre-ACT UP lesbians," Schulman writes, *had difficulty finding efficient, empowering tactics, setting winnable concrete goals, and having a clear idea who was supposed to be affected by our organizing efforts. There was something in the amorphous, generalized nature of our politics that guaranteed defeat. But it was only through ACT UP that [we] understood how to sequence political action. First make a demand that is possible. Then propose it brilliantly. When there is no response hold direct actions until your target is forced, through embarrassment or necessity to respond in some way and then work with them to see the proposal through, whenever possible. Not only can this kind of focus bring you closer to your ultimate goal, but it creates positive and satisfying experiences for fellow activists and motivation for strategizing for political change. I remember the first time I participated in an ACT UP demonstration where protesters sat in at government offices, and I realized that while the early eighties feminist movement encircled the Pentagon, we never walked in through its front door.*[35]

As Schulman's narrative demonstrates, an inadvertent association often takes place between being genderless and being male. The deconstruction of gender for "women" means that we are no longer "bound" by woman-based ideologies which "guaranteed defeat" in a male-dominated world; we, too, can have access to (male-dominated) public spaces and (male-oriented) political power.[36]

As Christianity adopts queer theory, we need to make sure we do not make the secular queer mistake of throwing away all need for God, religion, and spiritual life previously associated with the private sphere. Because we are all descendants of the nineteenth century, in America today religious work is often women's work; "women" are constructed as the people who have relationships with God, as the people who produce the necessary conditions for Christianity to exist. In deconstructing "men" and "women," it is vital that we not inadvertently disavow those things—like religion—that have historically been associated with women's sphere. It is critical that we hold up and take seriously the religious work that has been traditionally assigned to women, and that we understand that this is the work that *all* Christians must now participate in. As Christians, we need to resist the notion that the social reproduction of everyday life is menial work which only some should have to do. In the last generation, I suspect that many of us have learned to enjoy our children more than our mothers enjoyed us, (and to live with dirtier houses than they did as well); we have become adept at balancing our public and private worlds to enjoy both. If new Christian communities hope to be truly strong in the twenty-first century, they will need to valorize activities such as preparing safe and comfortable

dwelling places, cooking for others, teaching our children, being hospitable, praying, reading Scripture, thinking about the moral life, and organizing church activities. These tasks must be viewed as vocations that all Christians should undertake
regardless of their gender. While we Christians may not need the ontological categories of "men" and "women," we do need to recover and value the work historically assigned to women's realm. If we do not aggressively attend to recreating
"women's roles" in the new queer Christianity, we run the risk of losing our relationships with God.

From a certain angle, these strategies appear contradictory. Why focus on "women"
or women's sphere if that is the very category we are trying to free ourselves from?
Perhaps they are contradictory. But we need to live with this contradiction for some
while. We need to focus both *on* women and *beyond* them in order to prevent a new
queer Christianity from becoming another cover for the discrimination and disregard of women, and to keep spirituality in the picture. Queer theory can provide us
with interesting visions of a nongendered, politically progressive world, but only if
we recognize the need for feminist analysis as well. The church needs to attend to
both queer and feminist analyses if we hope to pursue more faithful ways of thinking about sexuality, gender, and spirituality. Queer discourse can help Christians
eliminate those categories that are fundamentally unhelpful in determining faithfulness. We no longer need to root our spirituality in gender; we no longer need to have
a certain kind of relationship with God based on whether we're male or female. Moving beyond the male/female binary will free us to receive God's love without attention to any other aspect of our being besides our primary and life-defining membership in the community called church. Such a move would also completely resolve
mainline denominational struggles around the issue of homosexuality; how could
we know if someone was "homosexual" or "heterosexual" if we had no recogniz-
able concept of gender? We also need feminism, however, to help us consciously focus on the "women's work" of spirituality and morality as central concerns in the
new queer Christian discourse. The church needs to actively remember those beings
constructed as "women" to remind us of the important work that has been done
throughout the ages that has helped us know God more fully.

In the last chapter I argued that gay Christian activists ought to look beyond the
struggle for gay marriage, because the heterosexual practice of marriage often
forced us into family units that took our focus off of communal living and life in
Christ. In this chapter I have suggested that gay activists ought to look beyond the

fight for gay ordination. As long as we continue to rely on the category of "homosexual"—a category which assumes essentialized gender roles—there will always be hierarchy of "gay" and "straight," and gay people will always be marginalized. What, then, should gay Christian activists and gay-friendly Christians be doing to make the church more resonant with God's vision for the new creation? There can be no better way to execute progressive Christian politics in the church today than to launch a serious and in-depth discussion about sexual ethics. Christians of every political stripe today perpetuate the notion that sex has nothing to do with God. The church, as it currently exists, functions as a system or web of lies which produces silence, over and over, on the subject of moral sex. Even when congregations or denominations allow some of us to publicly recognize one certain aspect about our sexual partner (their genitals), they never let us speak about what, precisely, happens to our souls or our relationships with God during the act of sex. They rarely let us tell what sex has to do with spirituality. It that sense, even our most progressive, affirming, and reconciling churches double as closets for both "gay" and "straight" Christians. The central question of contemporary Christian politics today should not be "Should homosexuals be ordained?" or "Should homosexuals be allowed to marry?" but rather, "What does any collection of sexual practices have to do with the Christian life? How does having sex affect one's relationship with God and with the Christian community?"

CHAPTER SIX

Toward a Progressive
Sexual Ethic

It is a story familiar to all of us. Two people—a man and a woman—are given paradise, the garden of Eden, and told that the pleasures and riches of this kingdom are theirs forever as long as they do not eat the fruit of one tree—the tree of knowledge. In the interpretation that most of us today have received, eating the fruit of the tree of knowledge means doing something sexual. Adam and Eve, with the help of the serpent, eat the apple and suddenly, mysteriously, sexual activity becomes intrinsically suspect. They no longer wander about the garden happily unclothed but hide their nakedness from God and each other. As a result of their sin we, too, learn that we should not understand our own sexual appetites as good, but rather as dangerous impulses that must be curtailed. The apple has become a symbol for us of the depravity of our own flesh. Most of our ideas about sexual ethics are designed to stave off evil and ensure that when and if we have sex, we're doing so for the right reasons.

In the last chapter, I argued that in the present way we speak of sexual morality, sex has nothing to do with God. But in fact, from a broader perspective, sex has everything to do with God. That is, Christian ethicists, moral theologians, and religious leaders throughout the ages have spent an enormous amount of time and energy thinking about when sex can be considered moral and when it cannot. While this preoccupation with sexuality has produced many detailed rules regarding acceptable Christian sexual conduct, it has also served as the foundation for persecution of difference within the church. In this final chapter, I examine existing systems of sexual ethics and the thinking about sexuality that lies behind them. Although some of the church's teachings have led to the disestablishment of women and gays, others offer momentous insights about when and how our sexual activity is pleasing to God. This chapter sifts through the tradition, retaining what is helpful in constructing a sexual ethic focused on God and jettisoning those things designed primarily to keep sexual and gender identities in outdated, oppressive hierarchies.

I suggested in chapter 1 that for many liberal Christians, issues of sexual preference fall under the umbrella of tolerance. Although the philosophical concept of tolerance has often helped curtail a great deal of human strife and suffering, it is not itself the heart of the Christian message. Liberalism tells us to tolerate one another, not to cause trouble for each other, but it does not tell us how to build Christian community across our differences. It does not tell us how to find peace and happiness in being together. As Jim Wallis writes in *The Soul of Politics*, "Liberalism is unable to articulate or demonstrate the kind of moral values that must undergird any serious movement of social transformation [because] the critical link between personal activity and societal change is missing."[1] Being tolerant is not enough; the gospel calls us not simply to put up with each other, but to know each other, find joy in each other, and care for each other's needs. As Christians, we must not be blind to the differences of, for example, race, gender, class, or sexual preference; rather we are instructed to learn more about what makes our brothers and sisters different and to build a stronger Christian community based on those differences.[2]

The liberalism and progressiveness of the 1960s enabled the prophetic voices of women, blacks, gays, lesbians, and other minorities to revitalize the church. Since then, however, a change has rendered the Christian Left less progressive and less vital. While Christians on the Left in the 1960s had positive visions of a good social order—world peace and racial integration, for example—liberal Christians today are less certain about how to articulate a positive social good. Where the liberal Christians of the sixties worked for concrete visions of Christian community and allowed pluralism to follow naturally, today's liberal Christians work toward pluralism and tolerance and hope that community will somehow follow. Although the social movements of the 1960s served as the basis for church renewal, the project has stalled; its promise has not been fully realized. I offer in this chapter a return to the roots of the Christian tradition's moral teaching on sexuality. This will not only help us clarify the role and importance of sexuality in our lives; it will also remind us of the radical call of the gospel. We can and should affirm new kinds of sexual relationships without abandoning Christian teaching, for that very teaching can help us avoid unethical sexual encounters in our new configurations.

In my search, I will not address some of the hotly debated questions in theology and biblical studies today. I am not interested here in whether the ancient worlds were bastions of hostility to the flesh as reflected in our biblical stories, or pleasure-loving worlds against which the early church rebelled. Similarly, I want to sidestep the debate over whether sexuality was thought to be sinful in ancient Israel itself or whether such an interpretation of Adam, Eve, and the Fall only emerged in later, patristic Christian teaching. I am not interested in investigating how sexuality came to be viewed negatively in the Christian tradition; and I am not involved in asserting the opposite, that every act and form of sex is essentially good and of God. Rather, I begin with the self-evident notion that sex—like most other activities in our lives—can be either good or bad. Sex is neither all good nor all bad, neither inherently moral nor inherently evil. Rather, a sexual act derives its meaning and morality from the conditions and circumstances that surround it. My task is to discuss the conditions and circumstances that delineate the differences between good and bad.

As Christians, we believe that many aspects of everyday life take on a different theological meaning in a Christian context. When we share a meal and break bread, for example, we understand ourselves to be invoking the spirit of God. Similarly, when we baptize our children and raise them, we understand that we are caring for beings that belong not to us but to God. Sex should be no different. While many ethicists concerned about sexuality have tried to develop systems of sexual ethics that would apply to all people regardless of faith, I am interested in how Christians understand and experience both sex and God. Under what conditions should Christians consider sex a good activity, and conversely, what are the marks of immoral sex? What parts of Christian history can help us think through these questions, and which parts simply reflect the misogynist, flesh-hating aspects of the ancient world?

As Steven Seidman and others have argued, any sexual ethic that attempts to direct all people at all times is both authoritarian and dangerous. In his work, Seidman demonstrates that different historical and contemporary cultures construct sexuality differently.[3] In some, sex signals romance and relies on strictly defined gender roles; in others, sex is an opportunity to escape those roles. For some communities, sex is a sign of ownership, for others a sign of radical equality. The ideas I outline here are targeted to the local community of Christians in America at the turn of the twenty-first century, to an audience that identifies itself as the church. I direct these ideas to those of us who have inherited a world of conflicted claims about sexuality: that our bodies are both good and bad; that sexuality is a God-given gift but the best way to know God is through celibacy; that even if God made us lesbian, gay, bisexual, or transsexual, he only wants us to live in heterosexual marriage. At the moment, our local churches and denominational structures are quite confused about what moral sex ought to look like; this chapter rediscovers and reinterprets the teachings of our tradition and applies them to the issues pressing our congregations today.

For most of us in the Christian tradition, sex is not just a simple genital activity but a symbolic one as well. It signals the fact that we are not isolated islands of embodiment but created to embrace others in physical relationship. Even when a sexual encounter occurs between ostensible strangers, the encounter itself very often creates a community or sense of meaning for participants. During sex, we often temporarily lose sight of our individual boundaries; we become united with another person in a way that changes who we are and what we hope for. We need to think about the morality of sexuality because sex links us, inexplicably but profoundly, with others. Sexual ethics is an attempt to define the mystery of companionship and belonging.

For twenty centuries, intellectuals have tried to define the role and function of sexual intercourse in the Christian life. From the early admonitions of patristic fathers like Augustine and John Chrysostom, through medieval scholastics such as Aquinas, to the more recent proclamations of many Roman Catholics, many Christian thinkers have asserted that sex is moral only when it is both unitive and procreative. Because these two terms help Christians determine when and how sex becomes moral and pleasing to God, and because they have such a long history in the tradition, it is worth exploring their meanings in depth.

The word *unitivity* denotes intimacy, steadfastness, and one-fleshness. In the unitive nature of the sex act, two are made one; the boundaries of either individual are blurred both literally and metaphorically, such that each individual becomes, at least momentarily a part of something larger than him- or herself. As Vincent Genovesi, S.J., describes it, "Sexual intercourse is a sign of total, unreserved giving of self. [During sex], the individual's personality is lost in an interpenetration of the other self." [4] During sex, people change because they merge with the body and spirit of another. As Lewis Smedes writes, "Sexuality is the human drive toward intimate communion. More than a mere physical itch that needs scratching, it urges us to experience the other, to trust the other, and to be trusted by that other person, to enter the other's life by entering the vital embrace of his or her body." [5] James Nelson similarly suggests that unitivity is: "the union of bodily, emotional, mental, and spiritual feelings in ways that we humans experience markedly positive sensations about the self. In sexual pleasure—be it lovemaking's orgasmic climax or in the deeply sensu-ous experience of breast-feeding one's infant—the body self feels profoundly uni-fied, taken out of itself and into another. . . . There comes a self-abandonment. The ego surrenders some of its control."[6]

This uniting with other souls that disrupts our isolation and individualism does not just take place during sex; it is the cornerstone of Christian community. The Bible calls us over and over to surrender our individualistic selves in order to become part of the Body of Christ. We are called to love each other in Christ even if that love costs us our lives. As Philip Turner states, "In Christ, Christians believe that it is no longer necessary to marry in order to escape loneliness. Baptism into Christ provides what was once provided only by marriage, and it is partly for this reason that the early Christians took the unprecedented step of saying that the single state was as honor-able as the married one and perhaps even preferable. Once baptized, each person is given both family and friends in such a way that the terrible problem of human loneliness is overcome by incorporation into God's family."[7] Thus, the Body of Christ is made possible only when we are able to transcend the boundaries of our own selves to become something larger, something part of God. Commitment to an-other, the tradition teaches us, is always more forceful when you feel that part of yourself lives in the other. Indeed, Rowan Williams goes so far as to suggest that uni-tivity is not simply a matter of wanting to be part of another, but also the feeling of having others want to be part of us, having the wanter and the wanted themselves be merged. It "is a transformation that depends in large part on knowing yourself to be seen in a certain way: as significant, as wanted."[8] Unitivity, then, is not simply an ethereal merging or an intimate connection between two selves. Rather, unitivity means we begin our moral reflection not with individual human subjects, but rather with the whole, the community, the Body of Christ. It is the understanding that our lives are part of and wanted by a larger communion.

Such unitivity entails risks of rejection, abandonment, and loss. Once we venture outside ourselves and locate life's meaning in the souls of others, we are no longer in control of our own destiny. Our lives, quite literally, are wrapped up in those of other people. As Karen Lebacqz states, "Appropriate vulnerability may be the pre-sentation for unitivity: without a willingness to be vulnerable, to be exposed, to be wounded; there can be no union. To be 'known,' as Scripture so often describes the sexual encounter, is to be vulnerable, exposed, open. Sexuality is therefore a form of vulnerability and ought to be valued as such. Sex, eros, passion are antidotes to the human sin of wanting to be in control or have power over another."[9] Thus, in unitivity, we overcome our desires to control both our own lives and the lives of other individuals in favor of a more organic representation of humanity. Unitivity is the understanding that we are never alone and that we are always produced by, in, and for a social context.

In traditional Christian thinking, the concept of unitivity alone was not enough to ensure that a sex act was moral and pleasing to God, since a unitive sex act itself might have little to do with God. For example, people of other faiths often expressed feelings not unlike unitivity about sex. What could guarantee that sex between Christians was unique and produced uniquely Christian results? The moral concept of procreativity filled this need. Procreativity dictated that every act of sex among Christians should be open to the conception of new life. Under the influence of natural law, procreation came to be seen as the logical, objective, and dominant end of sex, the reason behind the function.[10] Although not every sex act would lead to children, every sex act in the Christian tradition would welcome children as a way of confirming that the act was moral. Sex, when it was open to conception, offered to participate in God's grace by returning to God and the community a child, a new Christian. Thus, although the early church most often relied on conversion rather than procreation to attract new members, using procreation as a measure of sexual morality was a way to ensure that every sex act was indeed pleasing to God. Although the more subjective criteria of unitivity remained an end for all Christian systems of sexual ethics, procreativity insured that the unitive function of sex was accompanied by the more objective criterion of openness to children.

Thus, as late as 1968, the Roman Catholic Church affirmed that "every matrimonial act must remain open to the transmission of life. To destroy even only partially the significance of intercourse and its ends is contradictory to the plan of God and to his will."[11] The Roman Catholic magisterium continues to condemn abortion, as well as all forms of birth control from condom use to the pill to coitus interruptus.[12] These teachings have drawn severe criticism from many factions of the contemporary church. Some critics claim that this focus on procreation is a way for church leaders to devalue human companionship and to diminish and belittle the unitive aspects of sex, or to punish people who have sex (by requiring them to accept unwanted children). Many feminist commentators argue that the tradition's focus on reproduction is designed to keep women perpetually pregnant and further oppressed. While the focus on procreation often does function in today's culture in many of these negative ways, I propose that the intent behind procreation was not to belittle the flesh or to oppress women, but rather to make sex uniquely Christian by producing children who would become part of the larger church. Remembering that the intention behind this teaching on procreation was to involve both God and the entire church community in every act of sex will help us later to reconstruct an ethic faithful to this hope.

The more objective focus on procreation did, however, often overshadow the more subjective orientation toward unitivity. In legalistic abuses of the rule, the focus on procreation became a yardstick for measuring the morality of any sex act; if there was a potential for conception the act was acceptable, if there was no potential for it, the act was not. Thus, in some of the most blatant distortions of the teaching, adultery, rape, and incest were considered more acceptable (because they were open to conception) than activities such as masturbation, homosexuality, or heterosexual intercourse using birth control (because these activities were not). In recent years many moral theologians attempted to correct these distortions by placing equal or greater weight on unitivity. In some cases—as with the teachings of Vatican II—the point has been simply to affirm unitivity and procreativity as equal ends for the act of sex. Thus, the current teaching of the magisterium holds both unitivity and procreativity as equally important ends in any sex act. A sex act that is not unitive— such as rape or incest—is thus just as immoral as an act that is not procreative.

Other schools of thought have moved beyond narrow interpretation of procreativity, seeing it as including more than openness to biological reproduction. A variety of ethicists over the last sixty years have agreed that the philosophical concept of procreativity ought not to be limited only to conception. Beginning with the 1930 Lambeth Conference, in which Anglicans permitted the use of contraceptives in many cases, the moral weight of sex has shifted off of biological reproduction for many Christian leaders. As Roman Catholic ethicist James Hanigan writes, "The new life and love to be created and to be shared in [moral sexual relationship] must not be understood in the first place as the new child to be and the parental love extended to him or her. Rather, this new life and new love must first be seen as the new common life and love of the married couple themselves, which in Christian understanding, is but their participation in the divine love-life."[13] For Hanigan, then, procreation can be interpreted to mean the closeness that comes from sexual love as well as the conception of a child. Anglican ethicist Rowan Williams agrees: "If we are looking for a sexual ethic that can be seriously informed by the Bible, there is a good deal to steer us away from assuming that reproductive sex is a norm."[14] Similarly, evangelical ethicist Lewis Smedes makes the point as follows: "To make reproduction the essence and ultimate goal of sexuality is a put down of God's creation. . . . It is not as though sex is only a tool for procreation and not a gift in its own right."[15] Or, as Lisa Sowle Cahill states, "The old biological standard of procreative sex . . . has been widely judged inadequate to the full human experience of sexuality."[16]

This new consensus regarding the interpretation of procreativity stems from a number of different sources. First and foremost, many ethicists realize that contemporary life very often does not allow families to provide adequately for a large number of children. Families with more than four or five children are often at a serious economic disadvantage. Second, most moral theologians today recognize that the good of unitivity sometimes conflicts with the end of procreativity. That is, when the church requires every sex act to be open to children, many heterosexual couples are forced to forego the goods associated with sexual relations in order to limit family size. Such sexless marriages often hinder the kind of closeness that accompanies the feeling of being wanted by a spouse. Understanding that sex is good even when the couple is unwilling to have a baby is a way for that couple to achieve the end of unitivity without the burdens sometimes associated with reproduction. The wide acceptance of birth control in modern society has helped us see even more clearly the positive aspects of the unitivity that develops between a loving couple; an increased access to sexual intimacy without the fear of pregnancy often leads to a closer partnership.

Third, the focus on good parenting in the last fifty years has prompted many ethicists to make the distinction between the ability to *make* a new life, and the ability to *nurture* that life. We have learned that parenting is not simply a biological function, but an emotional and spiritual one as well. Thus, simply because a couple can biologically produce children does not guarantee that they will become adequate parents.

Finally, new reproductive technologies have made reproduction possible even without physical, sexual contact. Today, sperm and egg are routinely united in petri dishes; indeed, for couples who experience difficulty conceiving a child, in vitro fertilization is thought to be a more reliable and dependable method of fertilization. Embryos—along with sperm and eggs—are frozen for later use or for sale to infertile couples or individuals. Surrogate mothers carry fetuses for women who cannot (or will not) sustain a physical pregnancy. It no longer makes sense to think of sexual intercourse as the only means of acquiring a baby; therefore, it no longer makes sense to have openness to biological reproduction be necessary in every act of sex.

In an attempt to break out of the oppression associated with procreativity, some contemporary ethicists have exchanged it for the more flexible notion of complementarity. Complementarity is the idea that men and women possess different natures, which are designed by God to complement each other. For a man and a woman who love each other and seek unitivity, then, sex fulfills God's theological design by uniting these two differing, incomplete pieces into one whole being. Although the Roman Catholic leadership rejects this teaching, many conservative Protestants and Catholics have adopted it. Dominican ethicist Gareth Moore, for example, portrays the metaphorical thinking behind the proposition:

> If a man and a woman are complementary, they go well together. Together they form a pleasing or appropriate whole, and it is that larger whole that is incomplete without one of the partners. It is like strawberries and cream. There are those who think that strawberries and cream are complementary. Because of their respective qualities they go well together, enhancing each other and forming a satisfying whole, the cream offsetting the sharpness of the strawberries and these in turn cutting the bland fattiness of the cream. Cream without strawberries or something similar is hardly to be contemplated, and when strawberries are served without cream, there is something missing. The strawberries, nice as they are alone, lack something. But it is not that the strawberries are incomplete, lack part of themselves. They lack or need something else, cream. Without the cream, it is not the fruit that is incomplete, but the dish. . . . To say that men and women are complementary is to say that together they form a whole.[17]

Thus, for Moore, the complementarity of male and female leads to a whole that is larger and more complete than either of the components. James Hanigan speaks of the desire to achieve such a totality as a Christian vocation. In his view, the unitive wholeness achieved by a man and a woman lead to new life in God. When seen in conjunction with unitivity, then, complementarity guarantees sexual morality by bringing the whole of two-in-one fleshness closer to God.[18]

These assertions of complementarity are designed to free the heterosexual Christian couple from the criterion of procreation. With complementarity, it is no longer necessary to assume that every sexual union must be open to children, as each sexual union between a man and a woman is said to participate in the grace of God by making a whole, two-in-one flesh. For many Christians previously concerned about the size of their families, the move from procreation to complementarity as the objective measure of sexual ethics is an extremely liberating one. In these new formulations, the ends of unitivity and complementarity would rarely be set against each other; a heterosexual couple could act on their desires to become sexually united without feeling the pressure to be open to conception. Complementarity also helps combat the idea that sex—and flesh itself—are evil. Moreover, it releases Christian women from a lifetime of childbearing and child rearing into sexual relationships that can be fulfilling as a result not of the children produced but rather of the unification itself. In the move to complementarity, the end of unitivity can very often be more easily realized, as sex can be sought without the fear of unwanted children.

Although the examples just cited are modern ones, the foundations of complementarity emerged in the late nineteenth century, as a result of economic changes associated with early capitalism and industrialization.[19] It made sense in the second half of the nineteenth century to understand women and women's nature as radically different from and complementary to men's in large part because industry needed only about half of the nonimmigrant white population to join the workforce. The ideology that women ought to stay at home (and raise children and keep house) emerged in tandem with the fact that there were no jobs for them to go to. The ideology of complementarity—or as I called it, "gendered theology"—was an efficient way of procuring an employment pool while simultaneously ensuring the availability of God to each family member.

What is retained in the shift from procreativity to complementarity is the focus on God. The overriding concern in communities built on gendered theology, including those of the Christian Right, has been the desire to assure relationship with God. Undergirding complementarity is the idea that God intends men and women to unite sexually, and that such sexual unions bring the couple into a sense of wholeness and closeness to God. From the perspective of complementarity, God intends men and women to live together. Those who participate in male-female sexual relationships are fulfilling God's plan in a way that those who are not involved in a sexual relationship, or are involved in a same-sex relationship, are not. As with the norm of procreation, what is sought is God.

What is lost in the shift from procreation to complementarity, however, is the focus on the church community. Although complementarity does invoke the need for

Christian sex to be oriented toward God, it does not attend to the hope that sex also be oriented to or involved with the large community. Within the vision presented by complementarity, male and female together are complete and do not need the community of church to achieve relationship with God. Wholeness is achieved in this system not through acquisition of the Body of Christ but rather through reproduction of the nuclear family and the heterosexual, monogamous dyad. Indeed, as we have seen, complementarity or gendered theology, as the foundational thinking behind the family values campaign, supports the notion that the heterosexual nuclear family is the only acceptable way of life for Christians today.

The problems that accompany a Christianity based on complementarity are manifold. Although unitivity in sex might be more easily achieved with a focus on complementarity rather than procreativity, the idea that the only acceptable lifestyle for a Christian is heterosexual, monogamous marriage stands in conflict with much of our tradition, which valorizes both community and celibacy. Because the ideology of complementarity has greatly influenced our churches today, single people are often suspect. Without a Christianity based on a politics of community, there is little room in church for those not sexually involved with a person of the opposite gender. Singlehood is viewed as a liminal state, a holding pattern that occurs only on the way to the ultimate good of marriage.

The traditional goal of procreation emphasized not the completeness of the couple in the eyes of God, but rather the hope that sexual activity was pleasing to God and to the community. In the shift from procreation to complementarity, however, the ethical claims extended far beyond the realm of sexuality into assertions about what men and women should be. Thus, in this new ethic of complementarity, although all sex does not need to be procreative to be moral, all people do need to live in heterosexual dyads to be full members of the Christian community. In the more traditional teachings of unitivity and procreativity, although sexual intercourse needs to be open to procreation to be moral, any Christian could easily opt out of sexual intercourse by being celibate; such a lifestyle was considered both faithful and honorable. Because the focus of complementarity shifted from community life to married life, many of our churches today do not see celibacy as a valid option. In an ethic based on complementarity, a person is only complete when he or she is involved in a heterosexual marriage. Even though some moral theologians attempt to lift up celibacy along with complementarity, the result is unpersuasive; one cannot simultaneously assert that wholeness is achieved only through heterosexual union and that celibacy is itself also a desirable state. As James Nelson writes, "Singles frequently are thought of as less than whole persons since they are without partners. . . . Indeed, a voluntarily single life-style sounds vaguely un-Christian."[20] For this reason, I believe that single people are finding it harder and harder to find a home in many of our churches.

Additionally, the focus on complementarity makes sexuality the determining factor of a human being's relationship with God. It means that our theology is dependent on our genitals and on finding and sharing sex with someone who has genitals codified as "opposite" (despite the fact that science teaches us these things often exist in a range or continuum). In the ideology of complementarity, it is not that we understand ourselves as limited parts of the Body of Christ who only achieve wholeness with each other in community through the grace of God, but rather that each woman needs a man and each man a woman to ensure wholeness and relationship with God. As we have seen with the Christian Right, this thinking leads to a strong essentialism that pervades many aspects of theology and everyday life, an essentialism in which women are thought to be created primarily for a set of activities surrounding the home and children, and men for activities in the public sphere. In such a configuration, sexuality is the defining and limiting characteristic of human existence. Christians need neither church nor community to express faithfulness to God; they need only a strong marriage and clear prescriptions about how to act like a man or a woman.

Not surprisingly, the focus on complementarity also leads to direct criticism of homosexuality. If male and female together signifies relationship with God and salvation, homosexuality becomes a symbol of everything the Christian is not. Using the logic of complementarity, James Hanigan writes that "homosexual individuals are not called to a two-in-one flesh unity because they cannot become such a unity. They can become a two-in-one flesh unity neither ritually in the act of sexual intercourse, nor substantively in the new shared life in love of unity and difference that is male and female. . . . Homosexual relationships, because they lack the capability of becoming two-in-one-flesh signs of Christ's union with his Church, have been assumed in the Christian tradition to be inner-directed, selfish, non-vocational ways of life."[21] Thus, although the call for complementarity often makes unitivity through sex more accessible for heterosexuals, it also shores up the importance of both heterosexuality and rigid gender roles. Instead of a final outcome in which sex brings us closer to both God and church community, complementarity leads us to a God who is mediated through gender and to a church that is virtually unnecessary. Moreover, it overtly ostracizes gay and lesbian couples, other sexual minorities, and single people to the realm of less than whole beings.

Liberation theologians and ethicists interested in reversing this oppressive tendency have responded with systems of sexual ethics built largely or exclusively on the concept of unitivity. Discarding both procreativity and complementarity as normative for Christian sexual ethics, liberationists see the sexual acts of mutually consenting adults as moral because mutually-agreed-upon sex brings us closer to one another and to God and creates the conditions for justice by encouraging us to respect one another in every circumstance. Carter Heyward, for example, uses the concept of mutuality to suggest that sex involves both God and justice. In her definition, mutuality is the "praxis of relational particularity and cooperation which function as the way we know God."[22] Larger than traditional descriptions of unitivity, mutuality brings both merger and liberation from oppression; as she puts it, "It is not necessarily a happy feeling or romantic attachment. . . . It is the process by which we create and liberate one another."[23] For Heyward, the removal of control and oppression from the realm of sexuality through this focus on mutuality ensures that sex occurs only among consenting equals who create conditions of respect and justice for one another. For her, "the presuppositions that we live in a relational matrix with one another in the world and that we have a common response/ability to live in mutual relation provide the impetus for feminist/womanist liberation theology."[24] Thus, the ethic that begins with sexuality sets the example for a more just, ethical world.

In a similar vein, Anne Gilson suggests that God is present only when sex is mutual, when it is completely free of violence and coercion. For her, the unitivity achieved in mutually desired lovemaking is the way one understands God. As she writes, "Eros presents the opportunity to connect with ourselves, one another, the wider world, and God. In reclaiming and redefining erotic power, we reach out to the web of relation of which we are a part. Through erotic power we incarnate God in our everyday communities. Through erotic power we are able to unravel the multi-layers of self-hate. Through erotic power we are able to challenge the life-denying powers of injustice."[25] Thus, eros—or erotic love—becomes the sole foundation upon which sexuality is determined to be moral and through which God comes to be known. Eros additionally serves as the ground of justice, the event that leads to the dismantling of our oppression. In connecting through one another through eros, we experience the liberating love of God. As long as sex stems from eros and mutuality, it makes us more whole and brings us closer to God.

While the systems of Heyward and Gilson are primarily built on the traditional concept of unitivity and expanded to include a liberation-centered, coercion-free system of mutuality, the work of Christine Gudorf suggests that, because the Christian tradition has so distorted sexuality, we need to abandon all traditional formulations of sexual ethics—including unitivity—and locate morality solely in mutuality itself. As she suggests, "The Christian community [should] free itself from captivity to its theological and ethical tradition and experience more egalitarian, intimate marriages, more humane sex roles in society, and the validation of sexual pleasure." The new ethic here relies completely on a tradition-free sense of mutuality, on a self-evident sense of collaboration. As Gudorf theorizes it, "A Christian sexual ethic should make mutuality in sexual pleasure normative." [26]

In my reading, these appeals to mutuality (whether connected to unitivity or not) are an attempt to divorce sexuality from the power relationships that dominate most of our daily lives. While I am not opposed to this goal, I am not sanguine about its practical possibilities. All relationships rest on some configuration of power that makes a particular partner attractive. Whether it be the power to say "you belong here," to include the other in intimate moments, to define some things as sexual and others as asexual, or even in the power to suggest the possibility of a sexual encounter, power infuses every moment of every sexual encounter. It is not possible to escape that power even by an act of will. Indeed, although power limits the relationship on one hand, it enables it on the other. To think we can take politics out of sex (or out of any realm of daily life) is to miss the point of the many liberation movements that asserted—in no uncertain terms—that power is everywhere, that the personal is the political.

A second problem with taking mutuality as the norm for Christian ethics is the assumption that all people have relationships to their bodies whereby they know when they want to have sex and can be entirely free from coercion or influence. Such people would need to transcend communities, situations, and narratives, in order to determine their desires in an uncomplicated fashion. I suggest to the contrary that we live inside systems that form our desires, including our desires to consent to or resist certain sex acts. Culture, along with our perception and interpretation of our experiences, is what allows us to see and experience the world. What one community experiences as violence, for example, another may experience as sacri-fice. There is no foundational human experience of what sexuality is, but rather dif-ferent and competing interpretations of what it ought to be.

From a Christian perspective, the task of ethical inquiry is to figure out which of these desires are good for us and pleasing to God and which are not, and why. Con-sent alone cannot determine the value of certain acts and conditions. We often con-sent to things that may not be good for us or deny ourselves those things that would feed our spirits. Indeed, ethical thinking is necessary because our human wills are not freestanding entities that cannot be influenced, but rather are subject to manip-ulation by both good and bad ideologies. We need moral guideposts. For Christians, creating these guideposts means keeping one eye on the positive contributions of Scripture and tradition and the other eye on the vision of the world that God intends for us. From these two horizons, past and present, we derive our markers for Chris-tian sexual ethics. With them, we do not need to rely entirely on our will or our own desires to discern whether an act is moral or not, but can turn to the rightly interpre-ted teachings for external assurance.

Other gay-affirming works in theology and ethics ground their work in yet another concept: that gay, lesbian, bisexual, and transsexual people have special knowl-edge of God, that homosexuality necessarily entails a uniquely spiritual orientation. Corresponding to the liberationist impulse to give the "epistemological privilege" to the oppressed, these theologians argue not only that gay and lesbian people should be accepted by the tradition, but also that our spiritual constitution and in-herent natures allow us to know God more clearly than straight people do.[27] These works believe that recognition of the spiritual nature of homosexuals will lead to greater acceptance and understanding; they therefore trace the unique, spiritual contributions of gay people both inside and outside the church. From a Christian perspective, gay and lesbian people are good for the entire church because they can lead all of us closer to God. This line of argument is extremely dangerous. I resist the narrative that gays, lesbians, and other sexual minorities are spiritually oriented in a way that straight or celibate people are not, because such an assertion relies on the very distinctions I am trying here to challenge. That is, the major mistake of homophobic Christianity has been to think that solely because of their sexual pref-erence, lesbian and gay people have nothing to contribute to the church. However, the reverse proposition, that gays, lesbians, bisexuals, and transgendered people

—as a result of their natures—inherently have a special connection to God, is equally essentialist and problematic. It is to presume that every person who belongs to one of these groups absorbs the necessary experiences for such a task and that the accidents of sex and gender determine moral character (which is precisely the same assumption as the homophobic opposition). It is again to mark "gays" as different.

Furthermore, sexual preference and gender itself are not self-evident, self-interpreting categories but rather are constructed by a discourse or system that functions to serve some and to oppress others. Participating in that system from any angle is corrupt, even when the intent is to reverse the hierarchies. What we need to do, I suggested, is create and participate in a new and different system that challenges the way the world is currently factionalized by genitals and preferences. My proposal relocates the line of distinction not between gay and straight or male and female, but between church and world. I suggest we seek a system of sexual ethics that supports the new distinctions of church/world while actively disregarding the old, oppressive distinctions of male/female or gay/straight. We need to find a sexual ethic and ways of having sex that make us distinctly Christian and that clearly mark for us the differences between moral sex and immoral sex.

Some recent works in religion find hope in the nascent field of queer theory for such an ethical method. Although queer theory is a tool for helping us realize the constructed nature of sexual preference and gender identity as well as for helping us move beyond these identifications, it offers us little insight for ethics. Queers in principle are opposed to any ethical program that passes judgment on any sexual behavior. Because "queerness" in the pejorative sense has always been defined by its negative relation to a particular moral code, the new queer theorists today assert that it is time to eliminate the barriers presented by all moral codes. As Gayle Rubin writes,

> *Most of the discourses on sex, be they religious, psychiatric, popular, or political, delimit a very small portion of human sexual capacity as sanctifiable, safe, healthy, mature, legal, or politically correct. [A] "line" distinguishes these from all other erotic behaviors, which are understood to be the work of the devil, dangerous, psychopathical, infantile, or politically reprehensible. . . . We should [instead] judge sexual acts by the way partners treat one another, the level of mutual consideration, the presence or absence of coercion, and the quantity and*

quality of the pleasures they provide. Whether sex acts are gay or straight, cou-
pled or in groups, naked or in underwear, commercial or free, with or without
video, should not be an ethical concern.[28]

In essence, queers hope to make a place for alternative sexual expression that is completely free of the confining strictures of ethics. What makes sex good no longer has anything to do with procreation, complementarity, or unitivity, but is related only to what makes us feel good, what gives us pleasure, what we mutually desire and consent to. Thus, many aspects of queer culture show intense interest in alternative sex practices such as sadomasochism, pornography, and man-boy love, affirming in every case the perverse, the chaotic, and the nontraditional. Any ethical dicta that restrict, confine, or limit sex need to be challenged as part of the hegemonic force of dominant straight culture. Queer theory thus not only challenges the construction of male and female as "normal," but also disputes the idea that sexuality has any "normal" parameters at all. From their viewpoint, because sex itself is liberating, new and innovative ways of expressing sexuality are to be explored and encouraged. As Steven Seidman articulates it, "In challenging sexual object choice as a master category of sexual and social identity, queer theory suggests the possibility of legitimating desires other than gender preference as grounds for constructing alternative identities, communities, and politics. Hence, queer theory advocates non-conventional sexualities."[29] Thus, queer theory becomes loosely affiliated with issues and practices involved in exploring the boundaries of sexual pleasure such as sadomasochism, man-boy love, group sex, cross-dressing, leather bars, and other erotic subcultures. Queer theory is interested in affiliating with those communities that challenge the dominant notion of "normal," both in the construction of gender as well as in the act of sex itself.

While many of these works have shed a great deal of light on many gay issues, the agenda they advocate is—on this point—irreconcilable with the Christian tradition. As ethicists Patricia Jung and Ralph Smith note, "Christians have wisely taught that we cannot survive in a community where individual desire is the only criterion for appropriate behavior."[30] Our task as Christians, I believe, is not to deny the need for ethics in sexuality but to figure out how to make our moral systems more faithful to God and inclusive of all God's people. If our goal is to distinguish ourselves as Christians in order to combat other, unnecessary identifications such as gay, straight, male, or female, we need to work toward an ethic that helps us accomplish this.

What the church today needs is a way to recapture the intentions behind the early formulas of sexual ethics. Unitivity and procreativity in their earliest articulations were designed to make a public statement concerning sexuality within the Christian community. Sex for Christians would be something that not only drew the people involved in the act closer together; it would also draw them closer to God and closer to the entire worshiping community. While the appeal to complementarity solves some of the problems associated with unwanted children, it truncates the desire to tie sexual acts to the larger community and makes the heterosexual dyad the end in itself. While the liberationists' appeals to unitivity alone solve most of the problems associated with sexual oppression, the use of mutuality or eros assures connection neither to God nor to Christian community, as it relies on an independent and all-knowing subject who is bound by neither community nor tradition. How, then, can we use the event of sex to involve ourselves even more fully in God and in the larger community of the Body of Christ?

If the story of Adam and Eve and the apple is the impetus behind the concern that our sexual activity be pleasing to God, perhaps another story from the same book can help us puzzle out an answer to the problem. Many years after Adam and Eve, the earth is populated with both righteous and evil people. Two men are traveling in a strange land and wander unknowingly into a part of town known for its corruption. A good citizen takes them in and feeds them, but the folks in the neighborhood start harassing the house where the strangers are staying. These strangers should be more careful not to wander in to our territory, the neighborhood hoodlums reason to themselves. They start yelling; they want the men to come out so they can beat and abuse them; they believe they need to teach these guys a lesson about staying in their own place. Eventually, God intervenes and sends hellfire and brimstone down on the neighborhood, but not before the nastiness of the neighborhood has infected even the good citizen's wife.

This story, of course, is the story of Sodom, and it can teach us much about how we can be pleasing to God. Just as most of us have learned that the Adam and Eve story is about sex and original sin, so too have we learned that the story of Sodom is about a specific sexual sin: homosexuality. The "sodomites" are bad, immoral people because they want to rape the visitors. However, when the story is read more closely, the sins of Sodom are not sexual sins at all but sins of inhospitality.[31] Indeed, the author of the Book of Ezekiel corroborates this point. "This was the sin of your sister Sodom: she and her daughters had pride, excess of food, and prosperous ease, but did not aid the poor and needy" (Ezek. 16:49). Jesus as well admonishes, "Whosoever shall not receive you, nor hear your words, when you depart out of this or that house or city, shake off the dust of your feet. Verily I say unto you, it shall be more tolerable for the land of Sodom in the day of judgment than for that city" (Matt. 10:14–15). Sodomy is social injustice, inhospitality to the stranger. Although the Bible uses Sodom as a symbol of evil numerous times, none of these references refers to homosexuality.

Even though neither the Adam and Eve story nor the story of Sodom speaks directly about sexual ethics, they have probably had more impact on Christian thinking about sex than any other stories in the Bible. The fact that we have sexualized these narratives is interesting because they *can* bear new meanings about sexual ethics for a progressive church. While Adam and Eve can teach us that sex, like most aspects of human daily life, can be either moral or immoral, the people of Sodom teach us that what is ultimately pleasing to God about our sexuality is hospitality. If our sexual relations help us to open our hearts and our homes to lost travelers and needy strangers, they are good. And if they cause us to be aggressively territorial and abusive to outsiders, they are evil. Hospitality can be the new criterion by which we determine the morality of sexual acts. Rather than locating morality along lines of procreation, or along the lines of complementarity, we can now measure sexual morality by determining how well our sexual encounters help us welcome the stranger into our church and into our life with God. The original intent of ethical teachings about sexuality was to ensure that sex was pleasing to God by being open to new members joining the community of faith. Clearly, this can be accomplished by hospitality as well as by birth.

When I recommend hospitality, I do not mean that strangers need to be welcomed through sex itself. Examples of Christian hospitality exist all around us, from the shelters sponsored by Catholic Workers and local churches, to the way that newcomers are formally welcomed into local Protestant worship services. The work of the gay Christian activist Robert Goss shows how an intimate relationship can promote hospitality to the stranger. Goss writes,

> Generally, same-sex couples experience the need to share the fruit of their love
> with others. Their love finds the need to include others. . . . The more that [my

lover Frank and I] experienced the love of one another, the more we were freed to serve others in need. We took into our household ministry the throw-away people of our society, the developmentally disabled, alienated gay men and lesbians, and people living with the painful realities of HIV illness. We created a community of love for the marginalized and the disenfranchised.

The sexual fecundity of our relationship found further expression in forming an AIDS base community for HIV+ people, loved ones and friends. It was expressed in the founding of Food Outreach, a major AIDS service organization in St. Louis that provides meals and nutritional supplements to indigent HIV+ people. Compassion and the passion for justice characterized our covenant union and our ministry as a couple. When Frank was diagnosed as HIV+, I naturally involved myself with ACT UP, Queer Nation and several other organizations struggling for gay/lesbian/bisexual/transgendered civil rights. Too many of my friends had died of HIV complications, and too many of my friends had been the targets of violence, harassment, and discrimination because of their sexual orientation. It was a natural evolution of our covenant to grow in the social commitment to the justice-love of ACT UP and the gay/lesbian civil rights movement.

Our relationship is not atypical in the gay/lesbian/bisexual community. I personally know hundreds of long-term, stable couples who found the need to express their love in compassionate outreach volunteer services to the larger community and/or passionate commitment to work for justice. Their love overflows into the hundreds of AIDS service organizations, volunteer services outside of the gay/lesbian/bisexual/transgendered community, and the struggle for civil rights. Their love gave birth to compassionate outreach and a commitment to justice.[32]

Goss's writing captures the sense in which our lives in Christ need to be open to nurturing and caring for others. In this representation of his life, the focus has shifted from procreativity and complementarity onto hospitality, from unitivity with just one person into a holy union with his community and with God.

Unitivity and hospitality, it seems to me, are ways of talking about human life in a frame that is bigger than the individuated subject. Unitivity and hospitality provide us with a moral method that begins with the whole, with community, with collectivity, with the Body of Christ, and makes individuals only out of that material. In the frame of unitivity and hospitality, we are not self-contained, independent subjects with concrete and impenetrable boundaries; rather, we are social beings, part of a larger creation. We only know ourselves in relationship to and as part of the whole. In a Christian context, the moral markers of unitivity and hospitality remind us that any sense of individuality ought to take a secondary role to our membership in the Body of Christ. It is only out of the entire whole of Christianity that we emerge, and sexuality is one of many events that concretely push us outside ourselves. Sexual activity—when it is unitive and hospitable—is thus not a uniting of two "selves," but another instance of the whole, a nod to our wish for communion.

The community of faith can affirm this new ethic because it upholds the intent of the earliest methods while attending to the new cultural circumstances upon which today's church is built. The command to be hospitable can be seen as a part of the great commission to tell the world the good news of Christ. Our task in reconstructing a progressive sexual ethic is not to deny or sidestep power, but rather to invite others into the power of God, to welcome them into this radically transformative power which realigns the world, to see each other as Christians rather than as men or women, gay or straight, rich or poor. The new standard of hospitality advocates a union with all needing persons, and thus returns new life to the community. With hospitality, we have no way of condemning homosexuality because the very notion of same or different sex would fall away in favor of our common identification of Christian. Moreover, there will be no way to condemn what I have described as communal sex, for all of us as Christians would understand that sexuality that is hospitable—whether it is monogamous or communal—is good. Indeed, gay male and radical sex communities might even serve as models for explicitly Christian "experiments" in communal living and communal sex.

In the world of the Christian Right, gendered theology guarantees that all participants have a relationship with God. It is an intricately balanced philosophy built around the central premise that God is worth knowing, that theology matters. As such, gendered theology suggests that we cannot tamper with one end of it and expect the entire system to remain unchallenged. We cannot simply accept working women, gender equality, or even gay life without addressing how God will be reached and how relationship will be maintained without women at home full time. The religious work of women must be relocated somewhere else in the system. The emphasis on hospitality achieves this. With it, every Christian understands his/her task as that of making the stranger welcome in order to better know God. With hospitality, knowing God and greeting outsiders are no longer limited to the realm of women, and are taken up by all who identify as Christian.

Additionally, the new ethic of unitivity and hospitality challenges the historical distinction between public and private. Not only will women no longer be associated with home and domesticity and men with public spaces and work. The new ethic allows us to think beyond the public/private split altogether into a territory that strives toward the Kingdom of God. As we open our homes to outsiders and invite strangers in, our homes themselves become the more public space of church. Conversely, that which was once outside our homes now belongs to all of us, as the world around us becomes a place for community building and witness. There is no longer an internal realm for women to keep up and an external world in which men compete against each other. Rather, all genders are collapsed into Christian, and all Christians go about the seamless work of God. The distinctions to be made, under the new ethic, are not between public and private, male and female, or gay and straight, but between those working toward the new creation and those who are not. A new ethic based on unitivity and hospitality allows us to retain the best aspects of the tradition—the focus on union with partner, God, and community— while at the same time eliminating the oppressive tendencies associated with procreation and complementarity.

There are those who would argue that the church I describe here, where no distinctions are made between men and women or gay and straight, has little or no historical link to Christian history. To this I have one response. Our Christian church is an institution of change. My local United Methodist Church in downtown Durham has little in common with an antebellum slave church, which has little in common with a peasant-based medieval parish, which has little in common with a pre-Constantinian house church. Little in common save one thing: each of these organizations hopes that it is being faithful to God. Each is embedded in its own time and political circumstances, yet each responded as best it could to a God who calls us and acts in our lives. Our Christian church dwells not only in an historical past but also in the hopes generated by redemption in the future. As we move toward those hopes, we change.

Many of our denominations are in the unique position, at the close of the twentieth century, to join forces with gay, lesbian, bisexual, transsexual, and feminist communities in their struggles to end misogyny, homophobia, and AIDS. Our churches are called once again to end oppression. But it will cost us. We will lose membership, our houses will be divided, it might even become dangerous for us to attend worship. But it is this kind of church—one that dares to take prophetic stands in the face of hatred, discrimination, abuse, and misunderstanding—that most of us long for. It is time that we examine precisely what our sexuality has to do with loving God and being church. In doing so, we will be much better equipped to usher in the new creation.

Notes

Introduction

1. Quoted in James Findlay, *Church People in the Struggle: The National Council of Churches and the Black Freedom Movement, 1950–1970* (New York: Oxford University Press, 1993), 28.

2. Sex has become increasingly divorced from procreation in two ways. First, birth control is more and more accepted, even among many American Catholics. Second, more babies are conceived in vitro and through artificial insemination (by both husband and donor), outside the realm of sexuality.

Chapter One

1. Robert Wuthnow, *The Restructuring of American Religion* (Princeton, N.J.: Princeton University Press, 1988), 35.

2. James Davison Hunter, *Culture Wars: The Struggle to Define America* (New York: BasicBooks, 1991), 44, 118.

3. Wuthnow, *Restructuring of American Religion*, 138.

4. "Religious Right Goes for Bigger Game," *U.S. News and World Report*, November 17, 1980, 42.

5. Beverly LaHaye, radio talk show broadcast, April 17, 1992.

6. For a scholarly evaluation of the campaign, see John Green, "Pat Robertson and the Latest Crusade: Religious Resources and the 1988 Presidential Campaign," *Social Science Quarterly* 74, no. 1 (March 1993): 157–68.

7. Quoted in Bob Burtman, "Onward Christian Solders: Are Fundamentalists Waging War in Wake's Political Arena?" *The North Carolina Independent*, September 22, 1993, 11.

8. Quoted in *New York Times*, October 27, 1992.

9. It is interesting to note that while the mainstream media did report on stealth tactics on a few occasions, the story does not lend itself well to repetition. Once the strategies are uncovered for the first time, they cease to be "news." Thus, the mainstream media inadvertently helped the Christian Right fly "below radar" in these campaigns. Compare this, for example, to the extensive media coverage of Operation Rescue in summer of 1991 and 1992, which greatly helped to organize pro-choice opposition.

10. Erin Saberi, "From Moral Majority to Organized Minority: Tactics of the Religious Right," *Christian Century*, August 11–18, 1993, 781.

11. *New York Times*, October 27, 1992.

12. Tim LaHaye, quoted in "Whatever Happened to the Religious Right?" *Christianity Today* 33 (December 15, 1989): 44.

13. Jeffrey Hadden and Charles Swann, *Prime Time Preachers: The Rising Power of Tele-vangelism* (Reading, Mass.: Addison-Wesley Publishers, 1981).

14. Saberi, "From Moral Majority to Organized Minority," 784.

15. Grant Wacker, "Searching for Norman Rockwell," in *The Evangelical Tradition in America*, ed. Leonard Sweet (Macon, Ga.: Mercer University Press, 1984), 307.

16. See, for example, Robert Booth Fowler, "The Failure of the Religious Right," in *No Longer Exiles: The Religious New Right in American Politics*, ed. Michael Cromartie (Washington, D.C.: Ethics and Public Policy Center, 1992), 57–79. See also Michael Lienesch, *Redeeming America: Piety and Politics in the New Christian Right* (Chapel Hill, N.C.: University of North Carolina Press, 1993).

17. Cited in Marc Cooper, "God and Man in Colorado Springs," *Nation*, January 2, 1995, 8.

18. Cited in Donna Minkowitz, "The Wrong Side of the Rainbow," *Nation*, June 28, 1993, 901.

19. Cited in Cooper, "God and Man in Colorado Springs," 9.

20. Quoted in "Payback Time: Conservative Christians Support GOP 'Contract,'" *Christianity Today*, March 6, 1995, 43.

21. Hunter, *Culture Wars*, 114.

22. I am reminded here of James Findlay's wonderful portrayal of the National Council of Churches' courage in taking an early and unpopular stand against segregation. See his *Church People in the Struggle*.

23. Jim Wallis, *The Soul of Politics* (Maryknoll, N.Y.: Orbis, 1994), 44–45.

24. I am indebted here to June O'Connor's portrayal of Dorothy Day in relation to feminism. O'Connor cogently argues that although Day exhibited many virtues commensurate with contemporary feminism—such as belief in both interdependence and equality—Day did not support the first (1920) or second wave of feminism because she believed that middle-class women did not suffer from oppression. Thus, Day's "feminism" applied largely to poor women (June O'Connor, *The Moral Vision of Dorothy Day: A Feminist Perspective* [New York: Crossroad, 1991].)

Chapter Two

1. Linda Nicholson, *Gender and History: The Limits of Social Theory in the Age of the Family* (New York: Columbia University Press, 1986), 3.

2. It is also worth noting that political analysis (political theory) shifted from kinship structures to the public, economic sphere, thereby obscuring the activities that kept and keeps people in families. What cannot be questioned in this new economic structure is the activities and policies of the private sphere, especially those that keep the family intact. Thus this ideological system worked only as long as women "remained in their

place." I will show that when women challenge their assigned role, backlash tactics inevitably follow.

3. It is also important to note that other scholars trace the history of separate spheres in different ways. See, for example, Constance Buchanan, *Choosing to Lead: Women and the Crisis of American Values* (Boston: Beacon Press, 1996).

4. For an excellent account of this process, see Ruth Schwartz Cowan, *More Work for Mother: The Ironies of Household Technology from the Open Hearth to the Microwave* (New York: BasicBooks, 1983).

5. William Chafe, *Women and Equality: Changing Patterns in American Culture* (New York: Oxford University Press, 1977), 22.

6. A huge body of feminist literary criticism exists regarding the function and merit of this popular women's literature. For an analysis that favors nineteenth-century women's writing as an outlet for women's new sense of purpose and power, see Jane Tompkins, *Sensational Designs: The Cultural Work of American Fiction, 1790–1860* (New York: Oxford University Press, 1985). For arguments on the other side, see Nancy Armstrong, *Desire and Domestic Fiction: A Political History of the Novel* (New York: Oxford University Press, 1987), which proposes that women's sentimental literature functioned as an extension of the state; and Ann Douglas, *The Feminization of American Culture* (New York: Doubleday, 1988), which argues that sentimentalization served to denigrate both womanhood and Christianity. See note 16 on Douglas.

7. Barbara Welter, "The Cult of True Womanhood: 1820–1860," *American Quarterly* 18 (summer 1966): 151–74.

8. Carl Degler, *At Odds: Women and Family in America from the Revolution to the Present* (New York: Oxford University Press, 1980).

9. Nancy Cott, *The Bonds of Womanhood: "Woman's Sphere" in New England* (New Haven: Yale University Press, 1977).

10. Carroll Smith-Rosenberg, "The Female World of Love and Ritual: Relations between Women in Nineteenth-Century America," *Signs* 1 (autumn 1975): 2.

11. For a historiographic review of the literature, see Linda Kerber, "Separate Spheres, Female Worlds, Woman's Place: The Rhetoric of Women's History," in *Journal of American History* 75 (June 1988): 9–39.

12. For further analysis of the plight of black, poor, and ethnic women during the nineteenth century, see Ellen Carol DuBois and Vicki L. Ruiz, eds., *Unequal Sisters: A Multi-cultural Reader in U.S. Women's History* (New York: Routledge, 1990).

13. I am speaking here of social and political conservatives rather than economic laissez-faire conservatives. Rebecca Klatch (*Women of the New Right* [Philadelphia: Temple University Press, 1987]) does a wonderful job demonstrating that although these two groups have things in common, they diverge on many accounts, including and especially regard-

ing attitudes toward the sexual revolution. For economic conservatives, the rise of feminism is actually a positive development as it creates a larger labor pool and a stronger market. The social conservatives I examine in this book are less invested in economic independence and development and more involved with social structures related to gender roles.

14. Of course, women were not thought to be fully Christlike because as well as being more virtuous than men, they were also thought to be weaker, dependent, and more passive. These characteristics were the ones Welter objected to in "The Cult of True Womanhood."

15. Billy Sunday, quoted in William T. Ellis, *Billy Sunday: The Man and His Message, with His Own Words which Have Won Thousands for Christ* (Philadelphia: John C. Winston Company, 1914), 229.

16. According to Douglas's *The Feminization of American Culture*, as religion became associated with women, it simultaneously became less relevant to men. Although this might have been the case for some more liberal Christians, for evangelicals and conservative Christians the logic worked precisely in reverse. That is, it was because religion was very important that it was entrusted to women, (who were thought to have superior moral and spiritual constitutions). When women began to disassociate themselves from those roles, these conservatives and evangelicals responded forcefully, as we shall see.

17. The move to locate the spiritual lives of the larger body in only one faction of that population is not new to Christianity. Roman Catholics have long placed such authority in the magisterium, which holds the power to discern moral and spiritual behavior for all Catholics. Indeed, it might be argued that the paradigm of spiritual assignment can be found in the story of Jesus Christ himself, who did for all humanity what we could not do for ourselves. The same authority and sacrifice was inscribed in womanhood during the nineteenth century.

18. Jeanne Boydston, Mary Kelley, and Anne Margolis, *The Limits of Sisterhood: The Beecher Sisters on Women's Rights and Women's Sphere* (Chapel Hill, N.C.: University of North Carolina Press, 1988), 5.

19. See Nancy Cott, *Bonds of Womanhood*; Barbara Epstein, *The Politics of Domesticity: Women, Evangelism, and Temperance in Nineteenth Century America* (Middletown, Conn.: Wesleyan University Press, 1981); and Ann Douglas, *Feminization of American Culture*. Douglas's thesis additionally argues that the association between women and organized religion rendered American religion less influential. See also Mary Ryan, *Cradle of the Middle Class: The Family in Oneida County, New York, 1790–1865* (Cambridge: Cambridge University Press, 1981). In Ryan's account, men and women did not occupy wholly separate spheres, as both genders utilized voluntary associations for social life. Women and motherhood were simply the launching pad for the voluntary associations, which served as the central socialization tool of the nineteenth century. Similarly, Nancy Hewitt challenges the idea that antebellum women were confined primarily to the home. In her *Women's Activism and Social Change: Rochester, New York, 1822–1872*, (Ithaca, N.Y.: Cor-

nell University Press, 1984), Hewitt demonstrates that women's activity in the public sphere was as dependent on class as it was on gender.

While both Ryan and Hewitt persuasively argue that public and private spheres greatly overlapped, it is clear that the valorized sphere of domesticity was associated with women. Moreover, when women went outside the home to do paid labor or voluntary work, that work most often resembled tasks they had done in the home, such as nursing, teaching, and helping the poor. Although many of their efforts eventually fell under the more public aegis of "welfare rights," the origins of these efforts were strongly tied to women and to the work women did in the home.

20. It is also worth noting that before the Cult of Domesticity, the husband and father represented the family and spoke as the head of the household. Wives and mothers were at least abstractly figured into political analysis through the father's vote and representation (see Linda Nicholson, *Gender and History*). After the Cult of Domesticity, however, the man represented only himself (as an individual), and women were not present in the system at all. Because family life was politically irrelevant, women had little access to formal public representation. As we shall see, it was not long before women discovered and rebelled against this situation.

21. Jane Tompkins, *Sensational Designs*, 127–28.

22. In this chapter, I do not mean to make a historical correlation between conservative Christianity and any one particular denomination or religious movement. As several scholars have illustrated, even among self-proclaimed evangelicals, a wide variety of political positions exist, such that many evangelicals and even some fundamentalists may not agree with the ideology I classify as "conservative Christian." Rather than define the politics of particular fundamentalists or evangelicals, I intend here to delineate and explain the origins and implications of an ideology that is shared by and indeed organizes a large, amorphous group of Christians, many of whom participate in religion largely through popular media. For expositions of different political orientations involved in evangelicalism and fundamentalism, see Margaret Lamberts Bendroth, "The Search for 'Women's Role' in American Evangelicalism, 1930–1980," in *Evangelicalism and Modern America*, ed. George Marsden (Grand Rapids, Mich.: Eerdmans, 1984), 122–34; Grant Wacker, "Uneasy in Zion: Evangelicals in Postmodern Society," in *Evangelicalism and Modern America*, 17–28; and Idem, "Searching for Norman Rockwell."

23. In her *Desire and Domestic Fiction*, Nancy Armstrong makes the case that the drives for domesticity were regulated by the narratives embedded in popular novels; that is, that women learned their new social roles by identifying with fictional characters. Thus, the study of political history, according to Armstrong, ought not to be abstracted from the study of fiction; popular novels themselves caused and regulated these changes. In particular, Armstrong claims that we ought to look at the fiction that women read to better understand how the Cult of True Womanhood developed. I agree with Armstrong's analysis and suggest additionally that theological configurations also engendered and perpetuated domesticity. Both men and women learned and accepted their new cultural roles

through massive reinterpretations of both the bible and Christian history. Sermons, Sunday schools, and pamphlets generated and reinforced the Cult of Domesticity by offering nineteenth-century Christians narratives that portrayed the separation of spheres as the natural, Christian way of life.

24. Mary Ryan, "The Power of Women's Networks," in *Sex and Class in Women's History*, ed. Judith Newton, Mary Ryan, and Judith Walkowitz (Boston: Routledge and Kegan Paul, 1983), 167–86.

25. Douglas, *Feminization of American Culture*.

26. See Eleanor Flexner, *Century of Struggle: The Woman's Rights Movement in the United States* (New York: Atheneum, 1970).

27. See, for example, Boydston, Kelley, and Margolis, *Limits of Sisterhood*.

28. Carroll Smith-Rosenberg, *Disorderly Conduct: Visions of Gender in Victorian America* (New York: Oxford University Press, 1985), 245.

29. Kathy Peiss, *Cheap Amusements: Working Women and Leisure in Turn-of-the-Century New York* (Philadelphia: Temple University Press, 1986).

30. From *Kings Business* 12 (February 1921), quoted in Betty DeBerg, *Ungodly Women: Gender and the First Wave of American Fundamentalism* (Minneapolis: Fortress, 1990), 43.

31. For a careful rendering of fundamentalist criticisms of the suffragists and early feminists, see Margaret Lamberts Bendroth, *Fundamentalism and Gender* (New Haven: Yale University Press, 1993).

32. "Christianity and Woman," *Bible Champion* 32 (June-July 1926): 310, quoted in DeBerg, *Ungodly Women*, 45. For an exhaustive review of primary materials that persuasively support the thesis that fundamentalism was an attempt to recreate separate spheres, see especially DeBerg, *Ungodly Women*, chapter 2, "Conservative Protestantism and the Separate Spheres." See also Randall Balmer, "American Fundamentalism: The Ideal of Femininity," in *Fundamentalism and Gender*, ed. John Stratton Hawley (New York: Oxford University Press, 1994), 47–62.

33. Indeed, as DeBerg argues, fundamentalism attempted to return to the separation of spheres so vehemently that women were prohibited from occupying roles in church, a prohibition that was intended to relegate women solely to the home and to reify the differences between the spheres. As we shall see, other historians quarrel with DeBerg's interpretation of women's activity in fundamentalism.

34. See David Moberg, *The Great Reversal: Evangelism and Social Concern* (Philadelphia: Lippincott, 1977).

35. George Marsden, *Understanding Fundamentalism and Evangelicalism* (Grand Rapids, Mich.: Eerdmans Press, 1991), 67. As Marsden and others point out, however, the fundamentalist separation was not a full removal from society but "only a halfway separation

of most fundamentalists from the denominational mainstream" (67). In other words, fundamentalists relied on networks and organizations that transcended and cut across denominational boundaries. The broadly based use of media such as radio paved the way for the massive resurgence of Christianity via television in the last quarter of the twentieth century.

36. Alice Kessler-Harris, *Out to Work: A History of Wage-Earning Women in the United States* (New York: Oxford University Press, 1982). Kessler-Harris estimates that at least 3.5 million of these jobs were replacements for men.

37. Wini Breines, *Young, White, and Miserable: Growing Up Female in the Fifties* (Boston: Beacon Press, 1992), 10–11.

38. Gary Bauer, *Our Journey Home: What Parents Are Doing to Preserve Family Values* (Dallas: Word Publishing, 1993), 33, 46.

39. Breines, *Young, White, and Miserable*, 8.

40. Betty Friedan, *The Feminine Mystique* (New York: Dell Books, 1963), 7.

41. It is important to note that although she never acknowledged it, Friedan was speaking largely about a phenomenon specific to white, middle-class women. Later feminists have criticized her narrow focus. See Alice Echols, *Daring to Be Bad: Radical Feminism in America* (Minneapolis: University of Minnesota Press, 1989).

42. Friedan, *Feminine Mystique*, 13–14.

43. Ibid., 326. The strategy of self-awareness as liberation led to Friedan's second major work, *The Second Stage* (New York: Summit Books, 1981), a work which, in my opinion, articulated a version of the Cult of Domesticity. Gloria Steinem, in her bestselling *Revolution from Within* (Boston: Little, Brown, 1992), formulated a similar strategy of self-esteem as liberation. Indeed, it is interesting to note that feminist strategies of self-confidence and self-esteem often sound very similar to the rhetoric of women on the Right. For example, Beverly LaHaye argues that "as women, we want to know we are important and that we have a significant place in the world. We need to know that we matter to someone, that our lives are making a difference in the lives of other people, that we are able to touch their souls" (Beverly LaHaye, *The Desires of a Woman's Heart: Encouragement for Women When Traditional Values Are Challenged* [Wheaton, Ill.: Tyndale House Publishers, 1993], 20). To my thinking, feminist analysis ought to be more materially based. For a critique of Friedan's second work, see Ellen Willis, "Peace in Our Time: The Greening of Betty Friedan," in *No More Nice Girls: Countercultural Essays* (Hanover, N.H.: Wesleyan University Press/University Press of New England, 1992), 56–64.

44. Friedan herself went on to establish the National Organization for Women, and came to be associated with the mainstream strand of feminism. For an excellent critique of *The Feminist Mystique*, see Zillah Eisenstein, *The Radical Future of Liberal Feminism* (Boston: Northeastern University Press, 1981), 177–200.

45. Friedan, *Feminine Mystique*, 15.

46. As in the nineteenth century, it was not the theory of feminism or feminist leaders that the Right opposed, but rather the massive changes in American life, most especially women entering the workforce. The theorists of the 1960s paved the way for a new American lifestyle in which women worked (and consequently put men out of jobs). This second wave of fundamentalism is not attacking feminist theorists, but changes in lifestyle.

47. Marabel Morgan, *The Total Woman* (New York: Pocket Books, 1973), 36.

48. Ibid., 67.

49. *Chicago Tribune*, October 20, 1991.

50. Bauer, *Our Journey Home*, 36.

51. "The Maternal Imperative," interview with Brenda Hunter, *Christianity Today*, March 7, 1994, 15–17.

52. Contemporary conservative Christian texts often also prescribe which jobs or careers a woman should go into if she feels she must work. Again, these recommendations most often reproduce the work that women do in the home, such as teaching, nursing, and social work.

53. Susan Faludi, *Backlash: The Undeclared War against American Women* (New York: Crown, 1991), 402.

54. Indeed, Rebecca Klatch, in *Women of the New Right*, articulates this material concern even more strongly as she claims, "One of the most valuable property rights a woman now has is the right to be provided for by her husband; feminism [particularly ERA] will eliminate this right. Whereas now a wife has certain remedies if her husband neglects his responsibilities, such as purchasing goods on her husband's credit card and letting the store handle collection of payment, feminism will destroy such options"(136). In Klatch's understanding of conservative women, these legal protections were important because, as she suggests, "the underlying image of men is of creatures with uncontrollable passions and little common sense or loyalty. Only moral and legal authority can restrain the savagery of male nature" (138). This view of men, I suggest, stems directly from the way that male nature was constructed during the early industrial period under the doctrine of separate spheres.

55. Mrs. Ruth Bell Graham, quoted in Phyllis Schlafly, *The Power of the Positive Woman* (New York: Jove Publications, 1977), 72–73.

56. Beverly LaHaye, *The Desires of a Woman's Heart* (Wheaton, Ill.: Tyndale House Publishers, 1993), 7.

57. Ibid., 21.

58. Pat Robertson, "The Family and the Law," speech presented at the Family Forum II Conference, Washington, D.C., July 27, 1982.

59. Beverly LaHaye, *Desires of a Woman's Heart*, 32, 33.

60. Bendroth, *Fundamentalism and Gender*, 11. For other explanations of why women participate in conservative religious communities, see Susan Rose, "Women Warriors: The Nego-
tiation of Gender in a Charismatic Community," *Sociological Analysis* 48, no. 3 (1987):
245–58; Carol Virginia Pohli, "Church Closets and Back Doors: A Feminist View of Moral
Majority Women," *Feminist Studies* 9 (fall 1983): 529–58; Mary McClintock Fulkerson,
"Contesting Feminist Canons: Discourse and the Problem of Sexist Texts," *Journal of Feminist Studies in Religion* 7 (fall 1991): 53–73; and Rebecca Klatch, *Women of the New
Right*.

61. Bauer, *Our Journey Home*, 104.

62. As a result of this logic, several conservative "mega-churches" run in-house computer
dating services for unmarried congregation members. Mainline denominational "singles
groups" also participate in this logic when they cease to serve as support or social organizations, and function instead as groups solely designed to match unmarried church
members to each other.

63. Nicholson, *Gender and History*.

64. Indeed, most popular texts published by the Right, along with radio and television programs, refer to God as "father" with no apparent awareness of the inclusive language
debate. Although in these media, God is sometimes referred to as "creator" or "almighty
one," I have never heard a reference to God that was based on feminine attributes. For a
sophisticated, academic defense of the Right's use of the male language for God, see
Alvin Kimel, Jr., ed., *Speaking the Christian God: The Holy Trinity and the Challenge to
Feminism* (Grand Rapids, Mich.: Eerdmans, 1992). For theological defenses of the use of
inclusive language for God, see Elisabeth Schussler Fiorenza, *In Memory of Her: A Feminist Reconstruction of Christian Origins* (New York: Crossroads, 1983); and Rosemary Rad-
ford Ruether, *Sexism and God-Talk: Toward a Feminist Theology* (Boston: Beacon Press,
1983).

65. This relationship between men and God has inspired a great deal of feminist analysis;
see specifically Mary Daly, who claimed that "since God is male, the male is God" (Mary
Daly, "The Qualitative Leap Beyond Patriarchal Religion," *Quest* 1 [1974]: 21).

66. Jay Adams, *Christian Living in the Home* (Phillipsburg, N.J.: Presbyterian and Reformed
Press, 1972), 89.

67. Susan Foh, *Women and the Word of God: A Response to Biblical Feminism* (Grand Rapids, Mich.: Baker, 1979), 159.

68. Ruth Tucker and Walter Liefeld, *Daughters of the Church: Woman and Ministry from New
Testament Times to the Present* (Grand Rapids, Mich.: Zondervan, 1987), 258.

69. Bonnidell Clouse and Robert Clouse, *Women in Ministry: Four Views* (Downers Grove, Ill.:
InterVarsity Press, 1989), 20.

70.   Bendroth, *Fundamentalism and Gender*, 3.

71.   Michael Hamilton, "Women, Public Ministry, and American Fundamentalism, 1920–1950,"
      in *Religion and American Culture* 3, (summer 1993), 174.

72.   James Schaffer and Colleen Todd, *Christian Wives: Women behind the Evangelists Reveal
      Their Faith in Modern Marriage* (New York: Doubleday, 1987), 146, 87.

73.   Texe Marrs, *Big Sister Is Watching You* (Austin, Texas: Living Truth Publishers, 1993), 12,
      18. The government officials that Marrs refers to are Attorney General Janet "Johnny"
      Reno, Surgeon-General Joycelyn Elders, inaugural poet Maya Angelou, Secretary of Health
      Donna Shalala, Assistant Secretary of Housing and Urban Development Roberta "Bob"
      Achtenberg, and Supreme Court Justice Ruth Bader Ginsburg. It is worth noting that
      Marrs's main objection to these people is that they are all women who have overstepped
      their boundaries into the male domain.

74.   For example, the writers collected in Ron Lee's book, *A Scruffy Husband Is a Happy Hus-
      band* (Pomona, Calif.: Focus on the Family Publications, 1991), reflect on the difficulties
      that follow when the man is expected to be able to fix anything and everything around
      the house. See also Jack Balswick, *Men at the Crossroads: Beyond Traditional Roles and
      Modern Options* (Downers Grove, Ill.: InterVarsity Press, 1992) for a Christian work that
      tries to cope with the shifts in cultural expectations for men. For additional comments on
      the changing role of men in conservative Christian culture, see Wacker, "Searching for
      Norman Rockwell," 305. For a secular overview of the changing roles of men in society,
      see Lynne Segal, *Slow Motion: Changing Masculinities, Changing Men* (New Brunswick,
      N.J.: Rutgers University Press, 1990).

75.   Ann Douglas, in *The Feminization of American Culture*, made this argument for
      nineteenth-century Christianity.

Chapter Three

1.   Dan Quayle, *Standing Firm: A Vice-Presidential Memoir* (New York: HarperCollins, 1994),
      322, 326.

2.   Rush Limbaugh, *The Way Things Ought to Be* (New York: Pocket Books, 1992), 188.

3.   Bauer, *Our Journey Home*, 98.

4.   Ibid., 99.

5.   See, for example, James Dobson editorial, *Focus on the Family* magazine, May 1994, 10.

6.   Tim LaHaye, *Against the Tide: How to Raise Sexually Pure Kids in an "Anything-Goes"
      World* (Sisters, Ore.: Multnomah Books, 1993), 15, 13.

7.   "Teens Say 'No' to Pre-Marital Sex," in *Christian America* 5 (September 1994): 10. For in-
      formation on the larger organization, see materials from True Love Waits, The Sunday

School Board of the Southern Baptist Convention, 127 Ninth Avenue North, Nashville, TN 37234. See also L. A. Kauffman, "Virgins for Christ: Young, Hot and Herded to Purity in a Pop Evangelical Extravaganza," *Nation*, September 26, 1994, 306–9.

8. For a concise history of women and birth control ideology during this period, see Degler, *At Odds*.

9. Steven Seidman, *Embattled Eros: Sexual Politics and Ethics in Contemporary America* (New York: Routledge, 1992), 24.

10. Steven Seidman, *Romantic Longings: Love in America, 1830–1980* (New York: Routledge, 1991), 58.

11. James Dobson, *Love for a Lifetime: Building a Marriage that Will Go the Distance* (Sisters, Ore.: Multnomah Books, 1993), 37. For a sampling of other romance manuals, see Larry Crabb, *Men and Women: Enjoying the Difference* (Grand Rapids, Mich.: Zondervan, 1991); Norman Wright, *Holding onto Romance* (Ventura, Calif.: Regal Books, 1992); and Ed Young, *Romancing the Home: How to Have a Marriage that Sizzles* (Grand Rapids, Mich.: Zondervan, 1990).

12. As Rosalind Petchesky writes, "It is important to note that conservative ideology is not simply antisex; the point is not wholesale repression but the rechanneling of sexuality into patriarchal legitimate forms, those that reinforce heterosexual marriage and motherhood" (Rosalind Petchesky, *Abortion and Women's Choice* [Boston: Northeastern University Press, 1984], 263–64).

13. Stephanie Coontz, *The Way We Never Were: American Families and the Nostalgia Trap* (New York: BasicBooks, 1992), 23. Indeed, the marriage of young family members was crucial in these shows, as this was the only way of dealing with sexuality that the ideology had. As Coontz argues, "Young people were not taught how to 'say no'—they were simply handed wedding rings" (39).

14. Daniel Nicholas, "Pat Robertson: A Profile," *Religious Broadcasting*, February 1986, 65.

15. It is not coincidental that the Nickelodeon channel—a cable channel then devoted almost exclusively to 1950s reruns—gained national access in 1982, just as the family values campaign of the Christian Right was taking shape. Although Nickelodeon and other "family channels" have no financial link to the Christian Right, they doubtless gained audiences as a result of this turn to the "traditionalism" associated with the 1950s.

16. Quoted in Faludi, *Backlash*, 230.

17. Focus on the Family pamphlet, *The Year Was 1954 and We Were All Very Young . . .* (Colorado Springs, Colo.: Focus on the Family, 1994).

18. George Marsden, *Religion and American Culture* (New York: Harcourt, Brace, Jovanovich, 1990), 262.

19. Quoted in *New York Times*, September 23, 1980.

20. *Time*, October 21, 1991.

21. See, for example, Dr. James Kennedy, Mass Mailing letter, January 29, 1994. Coral Ridge Ministries, P.O. Box 407132, Fort Lauderdale, FL 33340-7132.

22. Quoted in Petchesky, *Abortion and Woman's Choice*, 265.

23. Seidman, *Embattled Eros*, 72.

24. *Time*, August 21, 1991, 28.

25. *Hotline*, August 26, 1991.

26. Dr. James Kennedy, Mass Mailing letter, April 15, 1994. Coral Ridge Ministries, P.O. Box 407132, Fort Lauderdale, FL 33340-7132. Emphasis in original.

27. For a more scholarly Christian examination of the relationship between Christian and American ideology, see Mark Noll, Nathan Hatch, and George Marsden, *The Search for Christian America* (Colorado Springs, Colo.: Helmers and Howard, 1989). These scholars argue that although Christianity has influenced and should influence America, it should not be called upon to run the government.

28. Jerry Falwell, *Listen America* (New York: Bantam, 1980), 104–05.

29. Randall Balmer, *Mine Eyes Have Seen the Glory: A Journey into Evangelical Subculture in America* (New York: Oxford University Press, 1989), 122.

30. For detailed analyses of how sexuality and gender organization construct other nationalisms, see Andrew Parker et al., eds., *Nationalisms and Sexualities* (New York: Routledge, 1992).

31. Although many conservative Christians today are both premillennialist and fundamentalist, the two logics are historically discrete. Premillennialist thinking has been present in many strands of Christianity since the time of Christ. Fundamentalism, on the other hand, is a more recent phenomenon arising out of the combination of nineteenth-century evangelicalism and antimodernist concerns, especially regarding biblical interpretation. Many premillennialists existed before the rise of fundamentalism; similarly, many fundamentalists exist who are unconcerned with biblical prophecy on the end times. However, most leaders of the contemporary Christian Right are both premillennialist and fundamentalist.

32. Many different types of premillennialism exist; competing factions disagree over the exact time, date, and/or order of events that will accompany the return of Christ. For sources that delineate the differences, see Timothy Weber, *Living in the Shadow of the Second Coming: American Premillennialism, 1875–1982* (Chicago: University of Chicago Press, 1983, 1987); and Stanley Grenz, *The Millennial Maze: Sorting Out Evangelical Options* (Downers Grove, Ill.: InterVarsity Press, 1992).

33. Hal Lindsey, *The Late Great Planet Earth* (Grand Rapids, Mich.: Zondervan, 1970).

34. Pat Robertson, *The New World Order* (Dallas: Word, 1991).

35. Robert Van Kampen, *The Sign* (Wheaton, Ill.: Crossway Books, 1992).

36. Grenz, *Millennial Maze*, 215.

37. Dr. James Kennedy, Coral Ridge Ministries, P.O. Box 407132, Fort Lauderdale, FL 33340-7132.

38. The Right employs two different argumentative strategies to denounce homosexuality. The first accuses gays of seeking "special rights" under the protection of civil rights. First conceived by Dr. James Kennedy of Coral Ridge Ministries, the argument claims that gays should not seek the rights accorded to minorities because homosexuals are not legitimate minorities. (They are not minorities because homosexuality, Kennedy claims, is a mutable characteristic—unlike race, ethnicity, and gender—and because there is no evidence that homosexuals suffer from financial discrimination or political weakness.) The "special rights" campaign has been extremely successful in marshaling black church and other support for antigay initiatives.

    The second strategy of the Right is to claim that certain passages from Scripture directly prohibit homosexuality. A wealth of information has been produced by biblical scholars on this issue. (See, for example, Robin Scroggs, *The New Testament and Homosexuality* [Philadelphia: Fortress Press, 1983], and John Boswell, *Christianity, Social Tolerance, and Homosexuality* [Chicago: University of Chicago Press, 1980].) In reading interpretations of these so-called antigay texts, it becomes clear that the Bible does not provide, in and of itself, a decisive ethical opinion on homosexuality.

    Arguments based on both "special rights" and Scripture, in my opinion, are not the foundational reasons for the Right's opposition to homosexuality, but rather a sort of shorthand for an orientation toward sexuality and God that runs much deeper. I attempt to delineate the logic of this orientation in the remainder of this chapter.

39. Gregg Albers, *Plague in Our Midst: Sexuality, AIDS and the Christian Family* (Lafayette, La.: Huntington House, 1988), 17.

40. Patrick Buchanan, *New York Post*, May 24, 1983.

41. F. LaGard Smith, *Sodom's Second Coming: What You Need to Know about the Deadly Assault* (Eugene, Ore.: Harvest House Publishers, 1993), 211, 215.

42. George Grant and Mark Horne, *Legislating Immorality* (Chicago: Moody Press, 1993), 131. See also idem, *Unnatural Affections: The Impuritan Ethic of Homosexuality and the Modern Church* (Franklin, Tenn.: Legacy Press, 1991).

43. Michael Fumento, *The Myth of Heterosexual AIDS* (New York: BasicBooks, 1990), 118; quoted in *The American Spectator*, February 1992.

44. Spenser Hughes, *The Lambda Conspiracy* (Chicago: Moody Press, 1993), 31.

45. Stanley Monteith, *AIDS: The Unnecessary Epidemic: America under Siege* (Sevierville, Tenn.: Covenant House Books, 1991), 20, 25–26.

46.   Albers, *Plague in Our Midst*, 34.

47.   Paul Cameron, speaking on *California Tonight* television show, January 16, 1987.

48.   Reported in *New York Native*, August 14, 1983, 9; quoted from July 12, 1983, news conference with Jerry Falwell.

49.   Spenser Hughes, *Lambda Conspiracy*, 23, 25.

50.   Grant and Horne, *Legislating Immorality*, 60, 64.

51.   On this point, see especially the film *One in Ten: The Kinsey Percentage, The Hidden Agenda*, 1993, distributed by Manhattan Center Studios, 311 West 34th Street, New York, NY 10001.

52.   Smith, *Sodom's Second Coming*, 15.

53.   From the film *The Gay Agenda in Public Education* (1992), published and distributed by The Report, T. Y. and Jennett Beeson, founders, 1-800-462-4700.

54.   See Lisa Duggan, "Queering the State," *Social Text* 39 (summer 1994): 1–14.

55.   John Ankerberg and John Weldon, *The Myth of Safe Sex: The Tragic Consequences of Violating God's Plan* (Chicago: Moody Press, 1993), 15.

56.   Monteith, *AIDS: The Unnecessary Epidemic*, 15.

57.   Grant and Horne, *Legislating Immorality*, 75.

58.   Connie Marshner, *Decent Exposure: How to Teach Your Children about Sex* (Franklin, Tenn.: Legacy Press, 1993), 31.

59.   Falwell, *Listen America*, 158.

60.   Indeed, historian John Boswell shows that this fear of being penetrated stems back to ancient Rome where "sexual passivity is popularly associated with political impotence." He states, "Those who most commonly played the passive role in intercourse were boys, women, and slaves—all persons excluded from the power structure. . . . A male who voluntarily adopted the sexual role of the powerless partook of the inferior status they occupied." Boswell argues that this abhorrence of passivity was transferred to the Christian tradition through the works of theologians and church leaders, and cites third-century theologian John Chrysostom's words as a key example: " 'If those who suffer [passivity] really perceived what was being done to them, they would rather die a thousand deaths than undergo this. For I maintain that not only are you made by it into a woman, but you also cease to be a man; yet neither are you changed into that nature, nor do you retain the one you had' " (Boswell, *Christianity, Social Tolerance, and Homosexuality*, 74; 157).

61.   From the film *The Gay Agenda in Public Education*.

62.   Beverly Wildung Harrison, "Misogyny and Homophobia: The Unexplored Connections," in *Making the Connections: Essays in Feminist Social Ethics* (Boston: Beacon Press, 1985), 135.

63.   Smith, *Sodom's Second Coming*, 245.

Chapter Four

1.   Jean Bethke Elshtain, *Public Man, Private Woman: Women in Social and Political Thought* (Princeton, N.J.: Princeton University Press, 1981).

2.   Barbara Dafoe Whitehead, "Dan Quayle Was Right," *Atlantic* 271 (April 1993): 48.

3.   Judith Stacey, "Scents, Scholars, and Stigma: The Revisionist Campaign for Family Values," *Social Text* 40 (fall 1994): 53.

4.   Mary Stewart VanLeeuwan, *Gender and Grace* (Downers Grove, Ill.: InterVarsity Press, 1990), 173–74, 171, 213.

5.   Rebecca Merrill Groothuis, *Women Caught in the Conflict* (Grand Rapids, Mich.: Baker Book House, 1994), 1, 110.

6.   Kath Weston, *Families We Choose: Lesbians, Gays, Kinship* (New York: Columbia University Press, 1991); Laura Benkov, *Reinventing the Family: The Emerging Story of Lesbian and Gay Parents* (New York: Crown, 1994); and Phyllis Burke, *Family Values: A Lesbian Mother Fights for Her Son* (New York: Vintage, 1993).

7.   Indeed, early secular feminists of the 1960s and 1970s argued that women's liberation was incommensurable and incompatible with the valorization of home life and domestic sphere. As Kate Millet profoundly states, "Patriarchy's chief institution is the family. It is both a mirror of and a connection with the larger society; a patriarchal unit within a patriarchal whole. Mediating between the individual and the social structure, the family effects control and conformity where political and other authorities are insufficient. Serving as an agent of the larger society, the family not only encourages its own members to adjust and conform, but acts as a unit in the government of the patriarchal state which rules its citizens through its family heads" (Kate Millet, *Sexual Politics* [New York: Simon and Schuster, 1969], 33).

8.   Rodney Clapp, *Families at the Crossroads* (Downer's Grove, Ill.: InterVarsity Press, 1993), 35, 35, 37.

9.   Ibid., 65.

10. Janet Fishburn, *Confronting the Idolatry of Family: A New Vision for the Household of God* (Nashville, Tenn.: Abingdon Press, 1991), 51.

11. See Phillip Keane, S.S., *Sexual Morality: A Catholic Perspective* (New York: Paulist Press, 1977); and Vincent J. Genovesi, S.J., *In Pursuit of Love: Catholic Morality and Human Sexuality* (Collegeville, Minn.: Liturgical Press, 1987).

12. Conservative critics of proportionalism would formulate the logic of proportionalism slightly differently by arguing that the committed relationship was the "lesser of two evils," thus suggesting that the proportionalists in fact sanction evil. Proportionalists would argue that the endorsement of committed, monogamous relationships is not an

evil but a good, because it carries with it the partial good of unitivity and avoids the evils of promiscuity and licentiousness.

It is also interesting to note that proportionalist methodology relies on a rather recent development in the history of sexuality, that is, that some people possess a "homosexual identity" that stands apart from practice, that gay people exist prior to and independent of sexual encounters. Thus, these texts do not suggest that gay people should make an attempt to go straight. Rather, they reason that if gay people cannot be celibate, they ought to be in permanent loving relationships in order to avoid greater sins associated with promiscuity. The idea of a fixed homosexual identity that operates independent of sexual practice is challenged in the next chapter.

13. Paul Ramsey was the first to develop this interpretation of procreativity as a justification for birth control. He writes that "a married couple engaging in contraceptive sexual intercourse do not separate the sphere or realm of their personal love from the sphere or realm of their procreation, nor do they distinguish between the person with whom the bond of love is nourished and the person with whom procreation may be brought into exercise." Thus, Ramsey argued that birth control is acceptable as long as the people engaging in sexual activity had agreed to be monogamous, that is, not to procreate with others (Paul Ramsey, *One Flesh: A Christian View of Sex Within, Outside, and Before Marriage* [Nottingham, England: Grove Books, 1975], 4).

14. Patricia Beattie Jung and Ralph Smith, *Heterosexism: An Ethical Challenge* (Albany, N.Y.: State University of New York Press, 1993), 146, 218. As Jung and Smith explain: "for gay men a surrogate mother is needed for artificial insemination with the sperm from one or both of the male partners in the union. For a lesbian couple either or both of the parents can have a child with artificial insemination. These ways of providing children in same-sex union, unlike adoption, link one partner in the union to the child biologically. . . . Surrogacy is certainly not solely the consequence of modern medicine. The biblical witness on marriage indicates that when wives were infertile other women could and did provide children. The story of Abraham, Sarah, and Hagar is the classic example" (218).

15. Ibid., 183.

16. John Shelby Spong, *Living in Sin: A Bishop Rethinks Human Sexuality* (San Francisco: Harper, 1988), 216.

17. Sidney Callahan, "Two by Two: The Case for Monogamy," *Commonweal*, July 15, 1994, 7.

18. These titles represent wings of mainline denominations' gay-affirming organizations (United Methodist, United Church of Christ, Lutheran, and Presbyterian, respectively).

19. J. Michael Clark, "Men's Studies, Feminist Theology, Gay Male Spirituality," in *Sexuality and the Sacred: Sources for Theological Reflection*, ed. James Nelson and Sandra Longfellow (Louisville, Ky.: Westminster John Knox Press, 1994), 227.

20. Frank Browning, *The Culture of Desire: Paradox and Perversity in Gay Lives Today* (New York: Crown Publishers, 1993), 77–78.

21. Paul Monette, *Becoming a Man: Half a Life Story* (San Francisco, Harper, 1992), 274.

22. For one lesbian's experience of these communities, see Pat Califia, *Public Sex: The Culture of Radical Sex* (San Francisco: Cleis Press, 1994). For a heterosexual perspective, see Lynne Segal, *Straight Sex* (Berkeley, Calif.: University of California Press, 1994).

23. Seidman, *Romantic Longings*, 186.

24. Browning, *Culture of Desire*, 80–81.

25. Clark, "Men's Studies, Feminist Theology, Gay Male Spirituality," 217.

26. Bruce Bawer, *A Place at the Table: The Gay Individual in American Society* (New York: Poseidon Press, 1993), 33, 254.

27. See Larry Kramer, *Reports from the Holocaust* (New York: St. Martin's Press, 1994). I recognize that in reality, the difference between these two patterns may not always be clear. For example, one partner of a monogamous couple might want to renegotiate the terms of the relationship in order to participate in such a community. We need to think about the differences between what I have called communal sex and those immoral practices signified by words like "lying" and "cheating." In my opinion, these discussions can lead us to better understandings of sexual morality.

28. Philip Turner, "Limited Engagements," in *Men and Women: Sexual Ethics in Turbulent Times*, ed. Philip Turner (Cambridge, Mass.: Cowley, 1989), 83.

29. Gabriel Rotello, "The Battle for Gay Marriage: What We Have to Lose," in *Out*, October 1994, 107.

30. Benkov, *Reinventing the Family*, 7.

31. Rowan Williams, "The Body's Grace," Michael Harding Memorial Address, Oxford University, July 2, 1989. (Published by LGCM, Cambridge, England, 1989), 4.

Chapter Five

1. Cited in Jeffrey Siker, ed., *Homosexuality in the Church: Both Sides of the Debate* (Louisville, Ky.: Westminster John Knox Press, 1994), 195. While chapter 5 displayed some of the limitations associated with gay marriage and notions of gay families, this chapter focuses solely on the debates surrounding ordination of practicing homosexuals and presents an alternative view, one that is not grounded in marriage, for legitimation of gay ordination. The Episcopal Church's logic helps us see how the two issues are deeply related.

2. Special Committee on Human Sexuality, "Keeping Body and Soul Together: Sexuality, Spirituality, and Social Justice," a document prepared for the Presbyterian Church (U.S.A.) 203rd General Assembly, 1991.

3. Cited in *The Church Studies Homosexuality: A Study for United Methodist Groups* (Nash-ville, Tenn.: Cokesbury, 1994), 7. The word *practicing* is chosen here to reflect the UMC's commitment to "fidelity in marriage, celibacy in singlehood," and, similar to the Episco-pal position, affirms homosexual identity while condemning homosexual practice. The word *self-avowed* is intended to avoid harassment of persons thought to be gay by third parties; it in effect mandates that gay clergy remain closeted.

4. For an exhaustive resource of mainline positions on homosexuality up to 1991, see J. Gor-don Melton, *The Churches Speak on Homosexuality: Official Statements from Religious Bodies and Ecumenical Organizations* (Detroit: Gale Research, Inc., 1991). For other resources that reproduce and discuss denominational documents, see Siker, *Homosexual-ity in the Church*.

5. Wuthnow, *Restructuring of American Religion*.

6. Mary McClintock Fulkerson, "Gender—Being It Or Doing It? The Church, Homosexuality, and the Politics of Identity," *Union Seminary Quarterly Review* 47, nos. 1–2 (1993): 30.

7. John Boswell, *Christianity, Social Tolerance, and Homosexuality*, 333.

8. Richard Hays, "Relations Natural and Unnatural: A Response to John Boswell's Exegesis of Romans 1," *Journal of Religious Ethics*, 14 (spring 1986): 200. Hays does express some doubt that "self-defined" homosexuals existed during biblical times; nevertheless, he believes that an act of "homosexuality" existed then that both Paul and we would recog-nize as such.

9. Richard John Neuhaus, "In the Case of John Boswell," *First Things*, March 1994, 56.

10. Two scientific studies are widely cited in the denominational literature. Simon LeVay's 1991 experiment found that the hypothalamus (the part of the brain thought to be respon-sible for sexual arousal and general sensitivity to stimuli) was smaller in gay men than in straight men. In 1992, Roger Gorski and Laura Allen found that the anterior commissure of the brain was larger in gay men than in straight men. Both studies have been criticized in the secular press, especially for the low number of participants on which the findings are based (LeVay used 19 gay men, Gorski and Allen, 34). For further information, see Simon LeVay, "A Difference in the Hypothalamic Structure between Heterosexual and Homosexual Men," *Science* 253 (1991): 1034–37; and Chandler Burr, "Homosexuality and Biology," in Siker, *Homosexuality in the Church*, 116–34.

11. Dorothy Williams, *The Church Studies Homosexuality* (Nashville, Tenn.: Cokesbury, 1994), 9.

12. One of the noticeable differences between conservatives associated with mainline denominations and conservatives associated with the mass-media Christian Right is the way each group treats the issue of changing one's orientation from gay to straight. For mainliners, although change might be desired, it is couched in language of forgiveness and in recognition that gross violations of human dignity often occur when we demand that gay people become straight. Mainliners also recognize that change is not always pos-

sible, even for those who desire it. For individuals associated with the Christian Right, the language is much more judgmental, the expectations harsher. In an era when groups like the Christian Coalition have a widespread influence over American Christianity, it is certainly difficult to sort out "mainline conservatism" from "far Right conservatism." It seems important, however, to make a distinction between rhetoric that suggests that homosexuals remain celibate (associated more with mainline conservatives) and rhetoric that suggests that homosexuals should "go straight" (associated with the far Right).

13. Richard Looney, "Should Gays and Lesbians Be Ordained?" in *Caught in the Crossfire: Helping Christians Debate Homosexuality*, ed. Sally Geis and Donald Messer (Nashville, Tenn.: Abingdon Press, 1994), 112.

14. Ibid.

15. David Halperin, *One Hundred Years of Homosexuality* (New York: Routledge, 1990), 30, 32. Because Halperin is not interested in studying women, he does not address issues of lesbian sexuality, and does not investigate the meaning behind heterosexual sexual activity that is designed to be procreative.

16. Ibid., 33.

17. George Chauncey, *Gay New York: Gender, Urban Culture and the Making of the Gay Male World* (New York: HarperCollins, 1994), 48.

18. Ibid., 65.

19. Eve Sedgwick, *Epistemology of the Closet* (Berkeley, Calif.: University of California Press, 1990), 2.

20. For relevant works, see John D'Emilio and Estelle Freedman, *Intimate Matters: A History of Sexuality in America* (New York: Harper and Row, 1988); Michel Foucault, *History of Sexuality*, vol. 1 (New York: Vintage, 1978); Steven Seidman, "Identity and Politics in a 'Postmodern' Gay Culture: Some Historical and Conceptual Notes," in *Fear of a Queer Planet*, ed. Michael Warner (Minneapolis: University of Minnesota Press, 1993), 105–42.

21. Sedgwick, *Epistemology of the Closet*, 8.

22. Ed Cohen, "Who Are 'We'? Gay 'Identity' as Political (E)motion (A Theoretical Rumination)" in *Inside/Out*, ed. Diana Fuss (New York: Routledge, 1991), 72.

23. See John D'Emilio, *Sexual Politics, Sexual Communities: The Making of a Homosexual Minority in the United States, 1940–1970* (Chicago: University of Chicago Press, 1983).

24. In my research on the mass-media Christian Right, I found only one reference to anything that resembled the concept of a firm biological or natural homosexual identity that existed independent of activity. (James Dobson made reference once to a "non-gay homosexual," which he described as "someone who has the orientation but remains celibate"; "Family Feedback" [*Focus on the Family* magazine, December 1994, 2]). All other mate-

rials of the Right agreed that homosexuality was a function of action and will, and could be changed.

25. From *The Standard* (published by Exodus International North America), 10 (fall 1993): 3.

26. Jerry Arterburn, *How Will I Tell My Mother?* (Nashville, Tenn.: Oliver Nelson, 1988), 5, 140–48.

27. Bob Davies and Lori Rentzel, *Coming Out of Homosexuality* (Downer's Grove, Ill.: Inter-Varsity Press, 1994), 38.

28. David Halperin helpfully comments on the fact that our own homosexuality often feels like it is rooted in nature: "Perhaps there is a sense in which the construction thesis is not only counter-intuitive but is necessarily so. The cultural construction of our sexuality is almost surely bound to be beyond the reach of intuitive recall. For our intuitions about the world and about ourselves are no doubt constituted at the same time as our sexuality itself: both are part of the process whereby we gain access to ourselves as self-conscious beings through language and culture. If we could recover the steps by which we were acculturated, we would not have been very securely acculturated in the first place, inasmuch as acculturation consists precisely in learning to accept as natural, normal, and inevitable what is in fact conventional and arbitrary" (Halperin, *One Hundred Years of Homosexuality*, 44). Thus, although the move to understand homosexuality may be counterintuitive to many of us, my argument here is that it would be a strategically advantageous move in relation to mainline denominational arguments regarding ordination.

29. Until recently, most feminists made the distinction between "gender"—which was thought to be culturally produced—and "biological sex"—which was thought to be inborn, natural, essential. In this view every person is *born* either male or female. Queer theorists today are challenging the naturalness of biological sex and dissolving both terms into cultural production. Thus, when I use the term *gender* in this chapter, I mean it to include the realm of characteristics we attribute to biology as well as those we attribute to culture.

30. Judith Butler, *Gender Trouble: Feminism and the Subversion of Identity* (New York: Routledge, 1990), 2.

31. See, for example, the widely cited essay by Suzanne Kessler, "The Medical Construction of Gender: Case Management of Intersexed Infants," in *Theorizing Feminism: Parallel Trends in the Humanities and Social Sciences*, ed. Anne Herrmann and Abigail Stewart (Boulder, Colo.: Westview Press, 1994), 218–37. The essay carefully chronicles many incidents of children born with some combination of "male" and "female" reproductive features, and demonstrates that physicians often make an arbitrary decision about which sex the child will become. Kessler is critical of the "incorrigible belief in and insistence upon female and male as the only 'natural' options" (218).

32. See Smith-Rosenberg, *Disorderly Conduct*; Lillian Faderman, *Odd Girls and Twilight Lovers: A History of Lesbian Life in Twentieth-Century America* (New York: Penguin, 1991);

idem, *Surpassing the Love of Men: Romantic Friendship and Love between Women from the Renaissance to the Present* (New York: William Morrow, 1981); and Adrienne Rich, *Blood, Bread, and Poetry* (New York: Norton, 1986).

33. Elizabeth Kennedy and Madeline Davis, *Boots of Leather, Slippers of Gold: The History of a Lesbian Community* (New York: Routledge, 1993), 12. See also Lisa Duggan, "The Trials of Alice Mitchell: Sensationalism, Sexology, and the Lesbian Subject in Turn-of-the-Century America," *Signs* 18, (summer 1993): 791–814. For an interesting essay which compares the differences between these two strands of lesbians in one geographic area, see Trisha Franzen, "Differences and Identities: Feminism and the Albuquerque Lesbian Community," in *Signs* 18, (summer 1993): 891–906.

34. It should also be noted here that the butch-fem lesbians have a much longer history of association with gay men than do the lesbian separatists invoked in earlier frameworks; coalition under the sign of queer is thus made much easier.

35. Sarah Schulman, *My American History: Lesbian and Gay Life During the Reagan/Bush Years* (New York: Routledge, 1994), 67–68. It is important to note that Schulman herself is sensitive to the sexist dynamic of new queer politics.

36. Additionally, the issues most often brought to the attention of the nation by popular queer actions are related to the AIDS crisis, and as one lesbian in the movement articulated it: "While the health crisis is a dire emergency that every thinking, caring person must address, it alarms me to see gay men blindly absorb women's caretaking without making much of an effort to reciprocate. The majority of gay men remain woefully ignorant about feminism, and too many are contemptuous of women's bodies and hostile toward lesbians. When I see a mass movement among gay men to raise money for breast-cancer research, or a volunteer army of gay men who are taking care of women with chronic and life-threatening illnesses, this resentment will be appeased" (Pat Califia, *Public Sex*, 25).

Chapter Six

1. Wallis, *Soul of Politics*, xvi.

2. The kind of tolerance that is promulgated in America today often assumes that white, straight, middle-class men are the norm, and deviance (and tolerance of that deviance) is measured by how far one moves from that point. That is, when someone claims to be "tolerant," they rarely mean that they are accepting of white, straight, middle-class men, for such acceptance would be, in most communities in America, a given. Rather, the concept of tolerance both notices and marks difference, and then takes the upper hand to "accept" those who are "other" (while those who *are* other are rarely in a social position to either reject or accept the dominant). Thus, the way tolerance is used today often reinscribes the idea that the normative or most common type of human being is white, straight, middle class, and male, and therefore often leaves underlying assumptions and oppressions untouched.

3.   Steven Seidman, *Embattled Eros*. See also Leonore Tiefer, *Sex Is Not a Natural Act* (Boulder, Colo.: Westview, 1995).

4.   Genovesi, *In Pursuit of Love*, 154. Genovesi's work locates unitivity almost completely in the "interpenetration of the moment of orgasm." I disagree with this assertion and believe that orgasm is only one of many sexual practices which may or may not produce unitivity.

5.   Lewis Smedes, *Sex for Christians* (Grand Rapids, Mich.: Eerdmans), 31.

6.   James Nelson, *Between Two Gardens: Reflections on Sexuality and Religious Experience* (Cleveland: Pilgrim Press, 1983), 37.

7.   Turner, "Limited Engagements," 81–82.

8.   Williams, "The Body's Grace," 3.

9.   Karen Lebacqz, "Appropriate Vulnerability: Sexual Ethics for Singles," in *Sexual Ethics and the Church: A Christian Century Symposium* (Chicago: Christian Century Press, 1989), 21.

10.   The natural law discourse that arose in the middle ages argued that the moral function of an organism or activity was intrinsically related to its final end. Thus, the final end of sex was thought to be not only the subjective feeling of the participants but also the objective goal of children.

11.   *Humanae Vitae*, July 29, 1968, Paragraph 14.

12.   In official Catholic teaching, the only form of conception control is the rhythm method, whereby a couple abstains from sex during the fertile periods of the woman's ovulation cycle. The magisterium allows this intervention because, in their thinking, it is not sexual activity that intentionally disrupts conception, but rather the lack of sexual activity altogether.

13.   James Hanigan, *Homosexuality: The Test-Case for Christian Ethics* (New York: Paulist Press, 1988), 90.

14.   Williams, "The Body's Grace," 8.

15.   Smedes, *Sex for Christians*, 37.

16.   Lisa Sowle Cahill, "Feminism and Christian Ethics" in *Freeing Theology*, ed. Catherine Mowry LaCugna (San Francisco: HarperSanFrancisco, 1993), 224.

17.   Gareth Moore, O.P., *The Body in Context: Sex and Catholicism* (London: SCM Press, 1992), 118–19.

18.   Hanigan, *Homosexuality*.

19.   Indeed, Anne Bathurst Gilson identifies the foundations of complementarity in a wide range of ethicists from the late nineteenth to mid-twentieth centuries, including Anders

Nygren, Helmut Thielicke, C. S. Lewis, and D. S. Baily (Anne Bathurst Gilson, *Eros Breaking Free: Interpreting Sexual Theo-Ethics* [Cleveland: Pilgrim Press, 1995]).

20. Nelson, *Between Two Gardens*, 96.

21. Hanigan, *Homosexuality*, 99, 97.

22. Carter Heyward, *Speaking of Christ: A Lesbian Feminist Voice* (New York: Pilgrim, 1989), 21.

23. Carter Heyward, *The Redemption of God: A Theology of Mutual Relation* (reprint of dissertation) (Lanham, Mass.: University Press of America, 1982), 17.

24. Carter Heyward, *Touching Our Strength: The Erotic as Power and the Love of God* (New York: Harper and Row, 1984), 16.

25. Gilson, *Eros Breaking Free*, 83.

26. Christine Gudorf, *Body, Sex, and Pleasure: Reconstructing Christian Sexual Ethics* (Cincinnati: Pilgrim Press, 1995), 25, 139.

27. For some examples, see Gary David Comstock, *Gay Theology without Apology* (Cleveland: Pilgrim Press, 1993); Robert Goss, *Jesus Acted Up: A Gay and Lesbian Manifesto* (San Francisco: Harper and Row, 1993); J. Michael Clark, *Gay Being, Divine Presence: Essays in Gay Spirituality* (Las Colinas, Texas: Tangelwuld Press, 1987); and John J. McNeill, *Taking a Chance on God* (Boston: Beacon Press, 1988).

28. Gayle Rubin, "Thinking Sex: Notes for a Radical Theory of the Politics of Sexuality," in *Pleasure and Danger: Exploring Female Sexuality*, ed. Carol Vance (New York: Routledge, 1984), 282–83.

29. Seidman, "Identity and Politics in a 'Postmodern' Gay Culture," 123.

30. Jung and Smith, *Heterosexism*, 103.

31. As James Nelson articulates it, "The story of Sodom was centrally concerned not with sex but with the injustice of inhospitality to the stranger" (James Nelson, *Body Theology* [Louisville: Westminster, 1992], 59).

32. Robert Goss, "Are Same-Sex Unions Procreative?" Webster College, St. Louis, Mo.